A MONOLOGUE IS AN OUTRAGEOUS SITUATION!

A Monologue Is an Outrageous Situation! How to Survive the 60-Second Audition is a concise guide for aspiring actors facing a 'cattle call' audition. Herb Parker proposes that in order for actors to stand out from the crowd, they must adopt the mentality that the entire play itself is an outrageous situation, requiring the characters to make equally extreme choices to survive. Understanding that monologues must have elements of the unpredictable, the fantastic and that which would never be done inspires actors to make choices that develop their work into a more personal, organic and exciting approach to performance. Through Q&As, tips, director's notes and a glossary full of outrageous actions, this highly accessible book shows actors where and how to find a monologue, edit it, and give the outstanding, impressive auditions that are most attractive to casting directors.

Herb Parker is Associate Professor in the Department of Communication and Performance at East Tennessee State University. He is a three-time recipient of the KCACTF "Excellence in Directing" Meritorious Achievement Award and a thirty-five-year member of Actors' Equity Association. He is the author of *BARK LIKE A DOG! Outrageous Ideas for Actors*, published in 2013 by Spring Knoll Press.

A MONOLOGUE IS AN OUTRAGEOUS SITUATION!

HOW TO SURVIVE THE 60-SECOND AUDITION

Herb Parker

Focal Press
Taylor & Francis Group

NEW YORK AND LONDON

First published 2016
by Focal Press
711 Third Avenue, New York, NY 10017

and by Focal Press
2 Park Square, Milton Park, Abingdon, Oxon OX14 4RN

Focal Press is an imprint of the Taylor & Francis Group, an Informa business

Library of Congress Cataloging in Publication Data
Names: Parker, Herb, 1954–
Title: A monologue is an outrageous situation! :
how to survive the 60-second audition / Herb Parker.
Description: New York : Focal Press, 2016. |
Includes bibliographical references and index.
Identifiers: LCCN 2015034449| ISBN 9781138120020 (hardback) |
ISBN 9781138120013 (pbk.) | ISBN 9781315651989 (ebook)
Subjects: LCSH: Acting–Auditions.
Classification: LCC PN2071.A92 P38 2016 |
DDC 792.02/8–dc23LC record
available at http://lccn.loc.gov/2015034449

ISBN: 978-1-138-12002-0 (hbk)
ISBN: 978-1-138-12001-3 (pbk)
ISBN: 978-1-315-65198-9 (ebk)

Typeset in Baskerville
by Out of House Publishing

For every young person who dreams of a career as an actor.

Merry and tragical? Tedious and brief?
  That is hot ice, and wondrous strange snow!
                                A Midsummer Night's Dream

CONTENTS

ACKNOWLEDGMENTS

I am grateful to Focal Press and Routledge for assistance in making this book possible, especially Stacey D. Walker, Meredith Darnell and Meagan White. I also wish to thank Christopher Owens, Producing Artistic Director of Virginia Shakespeare Festival; and special thanks goes to Mark Paladini, Casting Society of America and Head of the MA Theatre Program, Regent University, for perceptive and helpful counsel.

INTRODUCTION

Many years ago when I applied for entry into a national unified audition I found out that my monologue would be limited to just sixty seconds. One minute. At first I was scared to death, and then I was confused. "*Sixty seconds?*," I thought to myself. "That's *all?* How can I do a monologue in sixty seconds? How can I get it all in? It's not enough *time* to get up there and show them my stuff!"

If you have ever felt this way about an audition I hope this little book will help. It is meant to get you ready for such an audition, when you have just sixty seconds to prove to people looking for actors that you are good enough to be hired. The acting advice you will find here has probably been passed down over many years, from elder actor to younger actor, and because of this it has stood the test of time. It comes from a host of theatre people – actors, teachers, directors – who were kind enough to take me under their wing to pass along a combination of inspired wisdom and just plain common sense. Some of these thoughts have been told so often that they have become part of theatrical lore and might sound cliché, but don't let that scare you. If you have spent any time in theatre at all you will recognize many of them and may have heard them before, stated in different ways – in talking about motivation, for instance, some will use the word 'intention' while others might prefer 'objective' – but they are all trying to do the same thing. They are trying to make sure that once you have decided you are 'going for it' in search of a career as an actor you will have left no stone unturned in your odyssey of coaching and self-discovery. I try to pass these same thoughts along to my young actors today.

Though the focus here is on the sixty-second monologue there is another agenda, not just about auditioning alone but also hoping, in a small way – please forgive my lofty aspiration – to nudge you in the direction of life as a well-rounded person, whether you wind up in theatre or not. I can't help it; I think that's part of the journey, too.

I would like for you to use the book like this: imagine that we are sitting down together after you have worked on a monologue. I will then offer a few 'notes' about your work, which I ask that you take to heart and make your own as you apply them through trial and error, maybe finding a solution to a problem but at any rate leaving our session having been energized and encouraged to keep fighting ahead. Hopefully you will read and re-read the book for the other suggestions, for callbacks and private appointments in which your monologue can be longer – maybe as long as *two whole minutes* – as well as for tips on rehearsal and performance. As a quick refresher you might browse through them as you stand in line for an Equity Principal Audition outside of the Actor's Equity Building in New York, or as you wait outside of a prospective talent agent's office, or before going into a vast hotel ballroom for a national 'cattle call' audition. They might even help get you ready to audition for the very first time, whether for your high school senior play or for the first main stage show of your freshman year in college.

These ideas come from watching actors work, watching them sometimes struggle and occasionally stumble but finally from seeing them rise up and triumph. You might even be reminded of actors you have watched audition in the past. Remember what you thought? How at first you were suspicious of them but in the end you pulled for them? How your heart went out to them if they had a rough time of it or how you cheered for them inside when they did well?

Who knows? Maybe you will recognize *yourself* up there, toiling among them, living the dream of every young person who ever aspired to a life in the theatre.

What Is a Monologue?

A monologue is a long speech usually spoken from one character to another. A *soliloquy* is always spoken when the character is alone. Whether monologue or soliloquy such a speech comes out of some great need within the heart of the speaker. I suggest this:

1. Even if spoken alone, a monologue is *never* spoken to *yourself*.
2. A monologue is spoken out loud as a desire to fight for something *outside* of oneself, a need so great and far away that it cannot be reached otherwise. In speaking a monologue you are fighting to find the answer to some awesome question that has escaped you. You can say that it is an attempt to discover the *truth*.
3. A monologue is a monologue – that is, you *keep talking* – because you discover in the middle of it that there is *much more to say*. With every succeeding line, a monologue is a *discovery*.
4. A monologue is a continuing, unfurling of a truth that grows more ominous – or more *glorious* – the longer it goes on, therefore structurally it will build as you get toward the end. This build is built into the text by the playwright. The actor playing such a build can think of it like walking home after a long time away; as the view of your house comes into focus do you not gradually pick up speed and are you not nearly sprinting by the time you bound up the front steps to return to your beloved front door?
5. In Shakespeare monologues you are free to speak directly to the audience; in a contemporary realistic play you speak to the 'fourth' wall. However, whether realistic or presentational, whatever barrier or wall that may be in front of you,

your character's desire must be in effect to *reach out for human kindness.*

A play is about people caught up in an outrageous situation caused by love. In a monologue *your words* are an attempt to fight through that outrageous situation. During the equally outrageous situation known as the audition, your weapon is still those words, only in this case you are using them as you fight *to get a job.*

In a monologue you are driven to speak to another person about your troubles (or successes) because outside forces have *made* you. In a soliloquy these forces are the same only they are so powerful that you are compelled to speak aloud, even though *alone,* in an attempt to find rescue. That is why you are never 'by yourself' in speaking it. In both cases these speeches can be considered a 'cry for help' in a situation that might be characterized as outrageous.

Part I

PICKING YOUR MONOLOGUE

I would take plays and I would cut out all the other dialogue and make long monologues because I felt the other kids weren't taking it as seriously as I did.

Sally Field

1

AN OUTRAGEOUS SITUATION

I would like for you to begin your work with the following premise:

1. A play is about people caught in *outrageous situations caused by love.*
2. A monologue in a play is *an outrageous situation.*

You might ask, what do I mean when I say "outrageous"? Very simple. I am referring to the definition from Merriam-Webster: *Exceeding the limits of what is usual; not conventional or matter-of-fact; fantastic.* The word 'outrageous' has many contexts of course, and can suggest committing violence, dropping one's pants in front of strangers, foul language, toilet humor or other such things that gross us out depending upon the person hearing the word. When employed by the actor in rehearsal, though, I have found that it can almost immediately make the acting choices more *active.* An actor moved to do something *outrageous,* whatever this word may mean for them, is probably going to have at least an *image* of an act that is larger, louder and inherently more *dangerous* than the term 'conflict' inspires. Conflict is defined by Freedictionary.com as "a state of open, often prolonged fighting: a battle or war." This is not bad and it can be dramatically accurate. But what I like about the term *outrageous* is that it entails much more than fighting: it is about that which is sudden, unplanned, unexpected and unbelievable *even to the person doing it.* We humans are like this; it is the very stuff we are made of. Frazzled because of something entirely separate from the person we are speaking to we shout angrily at them, only to come back later attempting to apologize, saying "I am really sorry! I don't know what came over me!" Not knowing what has come over us is at the heart of dramatic characters and applied properly it can lead to choices more exciting than they might otherwise have been because they require more than just fighting a war. Outrageous choices make you do what you would *never do* even in the midst of fighting that war!

You must see monologues in plays as weapons to fight this war, to deal with the outrageous situations the story has placed its characters in. Monologues are *driven out* of characters, forced out of them as if against their own will. It is what happens to you, in the heat of an argument, when you have been finally forced to shout "I wasn't going to say anything, but—!"

And don't forget the vital second part to this premise. The actor must pair *love* as well as 'outrageous' to their character's story. Many years ago my acting teacher suggested to me that every play that has ever been written is about love. That's a pretty bold, broad, general statement, but think about it for a moment: *every* play that has ever been written is about *love.* Now think of plays that may have affected you; or a story that has moved you; or even a book or a poem or a piece of music that has touched you. Is there not some great, even if illusive, *center* to this piece of material that causes that material to rise above itself? Does it not affect you in some way? You do not need to have the language of either psychological or theatrical analysis to judge this; you only need to have the feelings of a human being. All you have to remember is that somehow, for *some* reason if you allowed yourself to be you were moved, you were affected, you might have even been brought to tears. In any event you were taken to some rare special place in your heart and soul that is unmistakable in its depth even though it might be difficult or frightening to attempt to describe. You do not have to agree with me but let me be bold to make a suggestion: it was *love* that made you feel this way. There are many kinds of love: romantic love, love of family and friends – love of *beauty*, that illusive beauty we find in all forms of art. What do you think?

To further illustrate this point let me tell you a story. One night two teenagers, whose families just happen to be at war with one another, meet for the first time at a party and fall into everlasting love. They marry in secret and before they can confess it to anybody the young man is goaded into a fight with his young wife's cousin, and because this cousin has just killed his dear friend the young man is infused with a hatred and desire for vengeance so great that he kills the cousin. The young husband is banished from the city and the only way his wife can join him is by escaping an arranged marriage to another man. The priest who married them – thinking that he is doing good – provides the young wife with a secret potion that will put her into a sleep so deep she will appear to be dead. In turn the priest will send word to the young husband what has been done so the two of them can escape. But the young man doesn't get the message and thinks his wife has really died. The young man buys a deadly potion and goes to the family crypt where she has been laid to rest. Once next to his wife's body the young husband drinks the poison, killing himself. At that very same moment the priest shows up, the young wife wakes up from the sleep she has been in, sees her husband dead and decides to kill herself, and does so by stabbing herself with her husband's sword.

Would you say that this story is *outrageous?*

And can you also make the case that it was caused by *love?*

Romeo and Juliet is about people who love one another and what they are compelled to do because of that love. Though you might be quick to complain "You're talking about some Shakespeare play 400 years old!" must I be forced to remind you of just how high the instance of teen suicide is in this country in the New Millennium? Of the instance of 'suicide pacts' between young friends and lovers? Of teen suicide due to bullying? These circumstances are truly tragic because they have actually happened, are more *outrageous* because they actually happened. Real life is far more crazy and unbelievable than the plot of any play. Once the actor can see the love and the outrageous situation in drama countless possibilities are opened up to them in other plays and even musicals: Willy Loman is in an outrageous situation as soon as he stumbles onstage with his heavy valises in *Death of a Salesman*; the African American Younger family are in an outrageous situation as soon as the matriarch buys a house in the all-white Clybourne Park neighborhood of *A Raisin in the Sun*; the musical *Wicked* introduces us to two girlhood friends who take outrageously different paths in the enchanted land of Oz; What about two hobos who meet each day at the same hour at the same place *waiting for* their third friend – *Godot* – to finally show up? The examples are endless, found in every theatrical genre, going back to the beginning of theatre itself when Sophocles started it all with *Oedipus the King* more than 2,000 years ago. Love can be found at the heart of virtually every human action; it is powerful, confusing, daunting, puzzling and glorious and we feel it even in its absence if we don't have it. Some of the most romantic sentimental people you know may have never had the joy of personally experiencing love and yet they know what it is like intimately because first they are human and second they have an *imagination*. The same is true of live theatre and plays performed onstage. Plays seek to express love in every iteration that people can encounter it: love found and love lost, love false as well as true – even love of material things (think of Harpagon' s comedic love of money in Molière's *The Miser*). In our weakness we even let ourselves get carried away because of the lack of love and so sadly we turn it inside out and then feel what we call *hate*.

Love puts us in outrageous situations.

Recognizing all of this can make the actors' choices just as big and almost as profound because they are coming out of the heart of a creature – you – who possesses more depth and complexity than fiction can contrive! Bolder, more risky choices are at your disposal as you rehearse and perform in plays. But do not mistake where I am headed with this; I do not mean to say that all of the work will be beautiful. For the actor love is not psychological or aesthetic, it is *earthy and provocative.* An outrageous choice is possible because we frail little creatures constantly do things that even we can't understand. Adding this to your monologue will help it to remain in and always be about the here and now, about breathing through our lungs and the blood that flows through our veins. Love is what makes you do what is outrageous and makes you willing to do it even if it kills you. It is why every playwright moved to compose a play for the stage has been possessed with this special love from the moment they picked up a quill or pen or tapped on a keyboard, trying as best they could to replicate it live onstage. What better engine to drive the dramatic comedic deeds of characters in a play than those plunged into outrageous situations?

Because a play is an outrageous situation monologues spoken in them must be as outrageous as the play in which they appear. This is true of comedy or tragedy and even musical comedy (in which a monologue is of course a song). We speak monologues because we are happy or in despair; it is simply the *need to speak* that is driving us. As such, monologues are never casual, they are never off the cuff or incidental. They come pouring out of us because we *must* tell someone – even tell the *air* when speaking a soliloquy – or we might explode. That's what directors and auditors are saying when they complain about actors they view in mass cattle calls not fighting hard enough for something. That fight is what they want to see you doing up there for sixty seconds.

A speech can be outrageous even, and especially, if it is quiet. Monologues need not be screamed out loud to make them outrageous; they only need to be driven by tremendous need. Think of when Hannah Jelks speaks of allowing a lonely disturbed man to hold her undergarment in his hands in Tennessee

Williams' *The Night of the Iguana*; of the consumption-wracked Edmund Tyrone ruminating about having never been born in Eugene O'Neill's *Long Day's Journey into Night*; of Hamlet speaking "To be, or not to be," Ophelia lamenting "O what a noble mind is here o'erthrown!" The same is true when singing a song in musicals. It ranges from the Von Trapp family singing the gentle ballad "Edelweiss" in *The Sound of Music* to the young Courier confessing the horror of war with "Mama Look Sharp" in *1776*, among countless other examples from the canon of musical theatre. To embrace a monologue as outrageous is not to make it over-the-top Greek tragedy; it is to recognize and seek to portray the weight and depth of feeling the human heart is capable of, which of course is limitless with a range as wide as there are humans to express it. The definition of 'outrageous' *incites action*. Even if, in rehearsal, the student goes too far in choices during their monologue and winds up doing what their character would not do, it is still helpful and instructive because they can discover for themselves first-hand what it is truly like to 'raise the stakes.' Which is what you must do in an audition that is only one minute long.

2

THE SIXTY-SECOND DILEMMA

The best possible way to be cast in a play is for a director to pick up the phone and call to offer you the job. They can do this because they have cast you before, you did good work for them and you did not cause any problems during their production. If your career has not yet reached this point you will have to go through what countless aspiring actors have had to go through before you. You will have to audition. This means you will have to prepare a monologue to perform for them to give them an idea of your talent and suitability for the play or plays they are casting. A monologue is required for audition across the spectrum of theatre in America, including Broadway, Off Broadway, Off Off Broadway, regional theatre, national tour, for theatrical agents as a means of introducing yourself, for community theatre, BFA and MFA university scholarship/assistantships, and of course for the season of university theatre productions.

We have never come up with anything better than the crucible that is the theatrical audition. For the performer it can be cruel and it can be humiliating; it can also be sexist, racist, and unkind to the overweight, the elderly and the disabled. But for the persistent performer it can also become the life-affirming experience upon which careers are made, and in any event we still do it because it is the best gauge we have, at a quick glance, of judging whether an actor we do not know is worth hiring.

One such audition you might need to prepare for is the mass, unified 'cattle call' audition sponsored by theatrical organizations across the country: Unified Professional Theatre Auditions (UPTA), University/Resident Theatre Association (URTA), Southeastern Theatre Conference (SETC), Straw Hat, etc., to name a few. These auditions are dedicated to providing time for as many actors to be seen in one day as possible, so they limit the actor's presentation time to between sixty seconds (if performing only a monologue) and ninety seconds (if performing a monologue and singing sixteen bars of a song). At first blush you might think – as I did many years ago – that sixty seconds is not enough time to present a fully realized dramatic performance. As a matter of fact you just might think that such a requirement is *outrageous.*

The constant complaint that I hear from colleagues when watching young actors audition is that during their monologues they are not fighting for anything, or if they are the stakes they are 'fighting' for are not nearly high enough. "Raise the stakes!" is the constant cry among my peers. Some of this may be because it can be hard to get young actors to make a big risky choice – the fear of looking foolish in front of one's peers in an acting class is powerful – but at least some of the problem is the sixty-second runtime. Sixteen bars of a song get you an extra thirty seconds but that doesn't help the solo actor.

Over time this seems to have led to the feeling, perhaps instilled by acting coaches trying to help, that since the monologue must be so short it is best to pick one that just gets the auditors attention by being *funny*. The logic is that "If I can make them laugh even a little bit maybe I will get a callback where I can use my *real* monologue to show them I can act!" You can understand how such a notion might seem best; auditors have been sitting in the audition room for hours and hours, they are no doubt tired and are losing patience listening to dramatic, over-loud speeches or under-key songs. The actor only has sixty seconds, so the solution must be to pick a monologue that is harmlessly amusing, more along the lines of a stand-up comedy routine than a speech driven by emotional human need. Right? After all, emotional human need *takes too long to establish*, they seem to be thinking. So just tell 'em a joke!

I have no problem with part of this idea as far as it goes. As a matter of fact I agree; in auditions where the time is greatly limited it is helpful if an actor can make their audience laugh. The problem with creating laughter alone however is that too often it leads to choosing material that in the end doesn't satisfy the full job of the actor. Auditors may be tired but they still want to witness a human being doing their best to get something from another human being. Those qualities are required for the lightest family fare as much as for the most sobering drama. Auditors gain no clue of your acting ability if you only tell them a joke or if the substance of your speech is limited to ruminating out loud "Did'ja ever wonder?" They might be moved to chuckle for a moment, but at that same moment they might well be crossing your name off their list because they can see only so many people before they leave town and therefore they must choose only those performers who are able to convince them that they can create characters of depth and range. This begins when they see actors courageous enough to fight for something up there!

The sixty-second audition is always remedied – I have seen it – when the actor dwells not on how short a time one minute is but rather on imagining how long it can *seem* to be. Only if you have ever 'gone up' on a line during a play – forgotten what you were supposed to say next – can you know this. Remember what it was like? How long those seconds – and they were always *only* seconds – felt like? How excruciatingly long it seemed before you were finally rescued by a cast member with a well-grunted hint whispered in your ear or for that errant missed line to finally come back to your addled brain?

Those seconds can seem just as long in a sixty-second audition. You don't need to be afraid that you won't have enough time to 'go thru' a journey.' What forgetting a line tells you that you can apply to a one-minute monologue is *time is relative*, it will also tell you that in your rehearsal process you will have to be disciplined. You cannot take all of the time in the world to react to a cue; because it will be necessary to edit your speech to fit into sixty seconds you will not have three or four images to express feelings, they will need to be paired down to one or at the most two. You will be making all of your beats and transitions faster but at the same time you are not allowed to rush. Rushing is a real danger because in addition to your speech it may be necessary to include your introduction and closing comments at the end. What will make your transitions 'faster' (and yes, they must happen faster) is making acting decisions motivated by tremendous need that drives you *forward*. This will also help you construct an audition monologue that adds variety to your one-minute performance.

And one thing more. This may not give you much comfort but keeping it in mind will be instructive as you work on your audition; the auditors watching you can tell whether they like you or not *even before you have opened your mouth*. The very moment you are moving to the stage they can surmise if you are nervous or self-confident, if you have been trained or if you are a neophyte, if you have been in a lot of plays or none at all, and yes, they can even hazard a guess as to whether, in their eyes, you are talented or not – almost *at once*.

You can always change their minds, though. As an actor you have been presented with a task that is twofold; you must present the Audition, which can certainly be characterized as an outrageous situation, and in order to succeed in that outrageous situation you are using a tactic that must be equally outrageous: the Monologue.

Sixty seconds need not be that great a challenge. Technically the time is brief, and must include your name and number in the bargain. It is therefore important to employ some helpful techniques as you choose, work on and present your monologue. In doing this you may discover that while your speech is by anybody's estimation very short, it can also be, for your purposes, just long *enough* …

3

WHAT TO LOOK FOR IN A MONOLOGUE

The list of audition monologue dos and don'ts are legion these days. To help you choose the best monologue for your audition let me speak in general terms about a few things.

Your Type

You must know your Type and make your monologue choice accordingly. This is one of the first lessons you will learn as an actor. It is hard but it is necessary that you accept it and even embrace it. Cynically, it is fair to say that you must *exploit* it. Your Type is what people think of you as you enter the room; it is the sort of actor they assume you will be when they first see you. I am not speaking about *stereotype,* in which the image of a person or thing is oversimplified to the point of the cliché. With Type I am talking about the stock categories that help storytellers tell their story. This has been the case since the beginning of time, since stories have been sought to be told. We desire to follow the fortunes of 'young lovers,' the 'romantic lead'; we hate the 'villain' and we laugh at the 'clown.' These roles can be played with as much depth as the playwright can provide and the actor can discover. It simply helps the audience to 'get' the story if the identities of the characters they view are clearly defined. People casting a play or a season of plays also abide by these rules, and your monologue is supposed to assure them of your place in the character caste system. The first few words of your monologue are usually enough to reassure them and by the end of it they will feel certain. If they think you are a particularly good actor they will give you a callback and ask you either to present more monologues to them so that they can get an even better idea of how wide your range is or they might offer you 'adjustments' to the speech they have just seen – little improvisations to see how well you take direction. For the most part – especially if the role they are casting is not as complex – as soon as they are satisfied that they know your Type they can then proceed. Your Type is your height, weight, body build, hair color, facial structure, the way you move and the timbre of your voice; it is literally everything about you that can be outwardly discerned and matched with a particular role in a play. It is *you*, how you were born and how you were raised, and it is as hard and fast as your DNA. Even if you do what most people would suggest you do in order to change your Type, if you lose a lot of weight and change your hair color, it will likely remain a rough climb to get people to think of you differently. Type is what you are even after all the training and experience have made you the actor/actress you are today and to change it you will have to expect a long period of self-examination – and worse: not being cast – before your transformation can be complete. If your lines of Type are not drawn boldly enough a director looking to cast a play in a pinch is going to have to think you're really great in order for them to 'find a place' for you in their show. If you can put up with this, good fortune attend your endeavors. As you will find, though, at least initially until a director gets to know your work the 'chameleon' actor who can transform themselves from role to role is actually pretty much a misnomer; they may be great once they get the job but because their look is neither one thing nor the other the hard part is getting that job in the first place.

The only other way Type gets transformed, and this unwittingly, is from the change of appearance brought about by having to lose weight to combat obesity and all of the ailments it can cause. That is different. In all things your health, mental and physical, must come first. As long as keeping your Type won't jeopardize your health it is best to embrace what you are with love and cool-headed, pragmatic salesmanship, otherwise you are going to be in for a rough time trying to find work as an actor.

When Type is firmly embraced and established you can go about the business of finding a suitable monologue, and there are rules you must follow. Please don't take offense:

If you are fat don't pick a stately leading man/woman.
If you look like the 'best friend/side kick' don't pick a hero/ heroine.
If you are young don't pick someone old.

This has nothing whatever to do with talent. Actors believe they can play any role, and sometimes they are right. But that does not mean they will actually get the opportunity to play those roles. In high school of course you will constantly see young actors – the tall ones or the chubby ones – playing elderly characters. And play them well. But don't expect these roles to be available to you once you enter the professional world. Again, unless an actor's range is known and cherished by a director, the only criteria – even before the question of how good you are – will be what you *look* like, and what role that says you are right for.

You are not only picking to Type because of casting; in addition to being about what you look like picking to Type is, by definition, *exploiting what you do best*. If you are talented as a comic, have an affinity toward the dramatic, speak language well, brood in realism best, etc., Type is the fusion of your looks plus your talent and if you are careful (and not hard-headed – there are legions of actors who stubbornly think they will do Hamlet or Ophelia someday!) you just might be able to 'Type' your way into working all the time!

What You Do Best

Your monologue must sell to the auditors what you do best. Know how well the particular monologue you have chosen will accomplish this. Take the time to study the sort of plays the theatres do; you are searching for the roles in those plays that you are right for. You must choose these kinds of monologues to suggest to the director, at least subliminally, the part you want in his or her production. You can do this once you are aware that the theatre company is doing a play you want to act a particular part in. Often for your first audition a director will not want to see you do a speech from the play being produced; this gives them the idea that you have your heart set on such and such a part. What is best is to pick a speech that is *like* the role you want to play; this allows them to see qualities they can find useful in another character as well as the one you are interested in. They can then hold off on dismissing you outright and consider you for other roles in the show. I should say, however, that if you are really good they will do that anyway, and in any event they might prefer you prepare something from the play for the initial audition because they are in a hurry to cast and need to get an idea of how you would fit the role sooner rather than later. Suffice to say that your monologue must sell your Type so well that it is as if, in effect, you are proclaiming "Whatever role you have that fits my Type *I* am the only one capable of playing it!"

Are you uncertain of what you do best? Is your experience not yet at the point in your career that you are clear on it? A big factor in deciding this is going to require you to look back at the roles you have done before. What parts did you seem to get cast in all the time? The lead? The best friend/side kick of the lead? The funny person? The villain? A smaller part that still had a memorable moment before the play was over? The only past roles you should not consider are the old-people parts I mentioned above.

Consider these factors in what you do best.

- Is the character close to you in age? Are they young and going through the travails a teen or twenty-something might usually go through?
- What do you honestly like about the character? Are you drawn to them because they are positive? Cynical? Witty? Weak?
- What caused you to pick the speech in the first place? Is there something they say in the speech that you have longed to say? Some imagery you wanted to express? Some burst of anger you wanted to display? Some moment of love you wanted to portray?
- In what way might the character be like you? Do you know 'just what to do' with the role?
- If they are not like you can you *imagine* being like them? Are you excited by the prospect of 'being someone else?'
- Were you comfortable in scenes that involved kissing? Or did you giggle too much?
- Is what the character wants relatively close to your own wants and desires?
- If not, can you *imagine* them being close to yours?

Ask yourself these questions as you remember the kinds of roles you have played. It is perfectly all right to choose based on what you enjoy and had fun doing – or even *think* you will have fun doing.

A Role You Can Play Now

Choose your monologue from a role you would be cast in right now. This must be based solely on the expertise and talent you possess at this point. Someday you may be ready to play a lead but if at present your skill is limited to the good supporting role it is best to stay with that. You will be taking your speech out of context anyway so perhaps you can choose from a leading character, but the 'role you can play now' rule is about roles you are *likely* to play, are likely to be considered for. The auditors watching you will be going through this mental process, as well. While you are up there you don't want them to think "This kid can't do that speech! They're not right for the part!" Until your ability has risen to the challenge stay within your own wheelhouse. Don't push yourself further than your ability is ready at this point to go. No one must be more hard core and cruelly realistic about the roles you can play right now than you because you want to get hired. A monologue must never be chosen because you hope to play that role *someday*.

Age-Appropriate

We have spoken about this already. The exception will probably be a character in their thirties; we accept that you can be this age because in appearance and energy young couples will not be that far removed from your own experience and capability. More difficult will be the young character man or character woman who played elderly characters to high acclaim before they were into or out of their twenties. Afterward, still baby-faced, they are plagued either by the 'you look old when you are young' or 'you are going bald but still have a baby face' casting problem. The only way to solve this is to find that young character monologue while you are young and pick the older character when you are older, or better yet look for a speech where the age of the character is not crucial. So if you are a millennial please don't risk the octogenarian with the crotchety old-age voice even if you played that sort of part and played it well. Now I can hear you suggest to me that this is the outrageous choice I keep harping about. That may be true. But I also want your choices, in addition to being outrageous, to be *smart*. The wrong choice is not going to get you cast and might – yikes! – even get you laughed at. And not in a good way.

Comedic or Dramatic?

It may be true that after having been put through the ordeal of actors shouting at them for six hours weary auditors will welcome a pleasant, relatively light respite from the *Sturm and Drang* of anxious actors. Comedy is such a respite. However, make certain that the speech is chosen from a genuine, full-length play, not from the single disembodied material found on some internet sites. Begin with these suggestions from among the fine playwrights working today: Neil LaBute, Sarah Ruhl, David Lindsay-Abaire (Pulitzer Prize-winner for *Rabbit Hole*) and Steven Adly Guirgis, who won the Pulitzer for his play *Between Riverside and Crazy*. These new voices in American Theatre will give young actors fresh material, whether the hope is to cause the auditors to laugh out loud or simply enjoy a broad smile. In some cases, though, be aware of the adult content of some of the pieces (Guirgis' *The M*********** with the Hat* is a prime example of this). Then of course an actor seeking the comedic should not forget the works of Neil Simon. Simon is the American Theatre's funny-line laureate, and he does it best because his plays are about put-upon people fighting for something in what for them is an outrageous situation. Therefore they work well when taken out of context. You are best, however, to avoid two of his plays: the terribly overdone "Mr. Cornell" speech from *Star-Spangled Girl* (and it is also a no-no because it requires a thick southern accent) and the "I like me" speech from his play *Chapter Two*. Otherwise have a good look at his other most famous plays: Oscar or Felix in *The Odd Couple* (the female version for you ladies, as well), the tortured young married couple in *Barefoot in the Park*, Eugene Jerome among other characters in *Brighton Beach Memoirs, Broadway Bound, Biloxi Blues,* and *The Prisoner of Second Avenue* and *The Last of the Red Hot Lovers* for you character actors. Christopher Durang is also good; just proceed with caution as well because some of his more acerbic sketches have also been added to overdone monologue lists (such as his "Tuna sandwich" speech from *Laughing Wild* and the "Tinkerbell is dead" speech from *Dentity Crisis*). Your comedic monologue will work best if your character is, at bottom, *likable, harmless and doing the best they can in outrageous situations.* The list of other playwrights for you to consider is extensive, including A. R. Gurney, Jr.; Ken Ludwig; Wendy Wasserstein; and Jean Kerr, Terrence McNally, Herb Gardner, Michael Frayn, Mary Chase, Lanford Wilson, John Guare and many others. Reaching further back into our American Theatre history you can also consider the writing team of George S. Kaufman and Moss Hart; their play *The Man who Came to Dinner* is sturdy as ever with fine speeches especially for women, and *You Can't Take It With You* continues to find enjoyable life in production, revived on Broadway to high acclaim with James Earl Jones in the role of Grandpa. A comedic speech need not be a laugh riot; it only has to afford us moments of simple humanity, allowing us to smile and nod at your human foibles. You could even glance at the role of Richard Miller in Eugene O'Neill's *Ah! Wilderness*, a love-sick, teenage, aspiring writer who gets into all sorts of scrapes. I would also add don't be daunted if in reading contemporary comedies you initially find it harder to see a 'true' monologue. Because of the fast-paced driving structure of comedy the plays may be composed of shorter scenes with back-and-forth-type dialogue, so in some cases be prepared to piece together a speech from a longer scene between two or more characters.

   If you choose a dramatic monologue it cannot be based on anger alone, causing you to yell at the auditors for the entire time (African American ladies please try to avoid the overdone "Sorry" speech from Ntozage Shonge's play *for colored girls* ...; a more contemporary choice with the same qualities is Lynn Nottage's play *Ruined*). If you suspect that a speech has value to you because it shows your ability to play anger, try as you work on it to base the motivation for that anger on *love*. Your performance must have changes that take your character – and *us* – through a course that will make you *different at the end than you were at the beginning*. In a performance with such change, your character, even in the throes of a serious moment, is allowed the time to laugh. Being able to do this might even offset the general preference for the comedic monologue in mass cattle call auditions, as long as you can show a crystal-clear transformation by the end of your speech. For dramatic choices begin first with American greats Eugene O'Neill, Tennessee Williams, Arthur Miller, Edward Albee, Lillian Hellman, Lorraine Hansberry and William Inge; and these are only a few – you will find many others. From play-wrights of today consider August Wilson, David Mamet, John Patrick Shanley, Jon Robin Baitz, Suzan-Lori Parks, Sarah Ruhl, Paula Vogel and Neil LaBute.

Who Is Your Audience?

Who will be your audience at the audition? A theatre company or individual director? What sort of show(s) will they do? Only straight plays? Only Shakespeare? Only musicals and light fam-ily fare? What are they casting? You must find out if they are casting a single show or a season of plays. It may be they will want to see more than one monologue; if they do not you must pick a speech that has (or into which you can build) enough changes of character so that they can see you go through a range of transitions and beats. Even if you are limited to one sixty-second speech you will almost certainly need a couple more monologues at the ready to show the companies should they call you back. This is when they want to really see what you can do.

I have listed unified theatre audition organizations in Appendix C in the back of this book. You can log on to each site on your own and check out the theatre companies who either will be attending future auditions or have attended them in the past. It may be that the majority of the companies are summer stock theatres that won't even be doing a drama. In this case it will probably be best to pick a comedic speech and – *if* you sing – a song. You can then keep the dramatic monologue in your pocket to show them even greater versatility if they ask "What else have you got?" at a callback.

What Roles Are Being Cast?

Does the director or theatre company have anything for you? This is related to Type but it is more complicated than that. If they are doing a season of musicals and you do not sing or dance you might be out of luck (although character actors: check out the specific musicals they may be doing if you can; there are a lot of good character roles in musicals that don't require singing or dancing). If they are doing Shakespeare and you are afraid of the language you may be out of luck there, too. If they are doing British drawing-room comedies and you do not have a viable British accent nor sense of the style you should avoid them, as well.

All of this said, however, I do encourage you to "screw your courage to the sticking place" as Lady Macbeth demands, and go to the audition anyway, even if you fear that you are not right for any of the roles. For one thing it is always a good idea to audition, even if it is just for the 'experience.' For another thing the auditors are, really, looking at *you*. You never know; somehow, *somehow* you might do something that catches their eye and causes them to take a chance on you. Even an unsuccessful audition – and by unsuccessful I only mean that you were not hired – can move you one step closer to that audition which will win you the job. It is actually possible to compel a director to cast you by the sheer force of your energy and determination as well as your talent. You truly never know.

4

WHAT TO AVOID IN A MONOLOGUE

With some monologues I ask that you proceed with caution, perhaps even avoiding them altogether in some cases depending upon how great or how limited the returns might be that you get out of them. Not all are off limits as such; it is simply that certain elements of them can be problematic, especially if they are to be used for a sixty-second audition. This is your call; a poor speech can be done well and a great speech can be done poorly but your agenda must not allow the auditors to think that much. Your only task is to impress them through the exciting and perhaps outrageous choices you make as you fight for the needs of your character. Why create more potential problems for yourself by allowing tired directors and producers the time to think? But you're the boss; it's your audition ...

The 'Challenge Yourself' Monologue

You must not experiment with a monologue at an audition. That is not the time to 'challenge' yourself. You are trying to stack the deck in your favor. This means minimizing your faults and maximizing your good points. Even if you are doing two speeches, such as classical and contemporary and/or dramatic and comedic, you are still not obliged to pick monologues beyond your range; your selections must be only material that you can hit out of the park! With all due respect sometimes acting coaches can fall in love with a sudden 'Let them know you're willing to *stretch* yourself!' notion about an audition monologue. They forget that they are not talking you through a breakthrough moment of discovery in class; they are coaching to make sure you 'give 'em a show!' when you get up there to audition. Your version of 'showing them your range' must be about giving the auditors a delectable taste of the breadth and width of ability you have *now*, not the wonderfully wide range you hope through training and experience to possess s*omeday*.

The Accent Monologue

Unless you are native born you must not choose a monologue that requires you to speak in a foreign accent. This is why rarely if ever do you see someone doing a speech from a play like *The Importance of Being Earnest*, and why the Brooklynese accent (as can be found in the plays of John Patrick Shanley, for instance) can sound so hopelessly mangled. You only have sixty seconds so why make your task harder with out-of-context material driven by culture and language, not to mention the lavish costumes and settings of British drawing-room comedies you won't have, either?

The Internet Monologue

There are internet sites out there where young actors seem to want to go these days to find monologues in a pinch. At these sites you will find a host of monologues to perform and in some cases they will even try to help you by including a list of generalized plot synopses and possible motivation for your character. For students desperate to find a monologue for acting class *tonight* they might be handy, but I would ask every young actor to refrain from choosing material from these sites, and here is why: most of these internet monologues do not have scripts; they are concocted speeches meant to *imitate* genuine dramatic feeling or comedy and because of this they can lack depth. You will need all of the talent you have to make one of these 'monologues' work. (The fact that you sought them in haste should tell you something to begin with. You must never try to find and memorize a monologue overnight. I have seen students who allow themselves to be put in such a jam despite my urging, yet they keep doing it and it always results in self-sabotage.)

To properly prepare your monologue it is best to read the play from which it came so that you can benefit from the Given Circumstances: what happened *before* your monologue, its full context and what made your character need to speak it, even though by definition you will be taking it out of context to perform it. Having this 'back story' even if you must change or re-imagine it can still enrich your monologue and your audition.

The other reason is more about me, admittedly, being *Pollyannaish* (definition: an excessively optimistic person). I would like to encourage every acting student to become more aware of the great plays written by some of the most gifted playwrights this country and the world has ever seen. Trust me, young actors, there is a reason – and I would like for you to know why – we are still producing and applauding plays like *Death of a Salesman*. Honest.

The 'Role You Have Played Before' Monologue

This can be very tempting – after all, you *have* played the part before and you probably still know the lines – but once again there is the trap of trying to re-capture context and moments that might have worked well in performance but which will fall flat without all the production values and full context that supported it when you did the role. Performance and audition have different circumstances and agendas. It is best to find a fresh new speech. If you feel that repeating a monologue from a show you've done before is going to benefit your audition at least do yourself the favor of completely re-thinking, re-vamping and re-staging it as a *new* monologue in a new context, driven not by tracing a character's needs over the course of two hours but instead motivated by selling how good an actor you are in sixty seconds *right now.*

The Phone-Call Monologue

Sometimes you might come across a monologue where a character is talking to someone over the telephone. Phone-call monologues only raise the question of "Who are you talking to?" because built into them is the constant need to *pause* as you listen to what the 'person' on the *other end of the line* is saying. With the usual monologue we accept that the person you are talking to is 'in the same room' even though we can't see them. The continuous halting in a phone-call monologue causes a hiccupping rhythm to the audition that prevents you from building momentum, so vital to an audition that is only sixty seconds long. The phone-call monologue can also present the 'mime' problem an auditioning actor must always avoid: the challenge of creating an object you do not have that your character must have. If too much attention is given to 'creating' the phone it might take you *away from the audience.* We might almost feel like we are saddled with waiting until you get off the phone, just like in real life. The point is the entire speech becomes more about the *phone* and less about *you.* Worst of all it can also result in demonstrating how well – or how poorly! – you are creating an *invisible telephone.* Neil Simon has written some wonderful, truly funny speeches in which his characters bemoan their outrageous circumstances over a telephone. Oscar Madison of *The Odd Couple* comes to mind for one, but don't forget Oscar has the theatrical context of props, lights, sets, etc. If you truly desire to use one of these speeches be very clear on what you want from the person you are talking to, and in rehearsal write down and memorize *every cue you believe they are speaking to you and make BIGGER reactions to them.* This might help you make it work.

The 'Feel Sorry for Yourself' Monologue

If you are an actress thinking of picking a dramatic monologue perhaps you have come across the work of Tennessee Williams.

Williams is perhaps the greatest writer of female characters in the history of the American Theatre, but monologues from some of his female characters (Alma in *Summer and Smoke*, Hannah in *The Night of the Iguana*, Amanda Wingfield in *The Glass Menagerie* and certainly Blanche DuBois in *A Streetcar Named Desire* among them) can be tricky because sometimes they can seem to be feeling sorry for themselves. To be fair most of them are great speeches, full of passion and repressed longing, but if the performer is not careful they can result in moments of dour mood rather than being about fragile people doing their best to overcome life's difficulty. Characters that wallow in self-pity doom your audition, especially when you are limited to only sixty seconds. Ladies, before you pick a monologue from one of these characters take the time to dig deep into the text so that you can perform, in addition to all of their despair, at least a moment, preferably more, of two things:

1. An objective that is fighting to *overcome* your circumstance.
2. *Laughter* as a *tactic* to overcome your circumstance.

Williams is not the only one guilty of the occasional 'feel sorry for yourself' monologue. A male version of this is the character Sammy Goldenbaum in William Inge's play *The Dark at the Top of the Stairs*, when he confesses to being lonely at military school, pining away for the actress mother who doesn't have time for him. Sammy commits suicide later in the play. The actor must not *telegraph* this in his monologue spoken out of a desire for hope and comfort. If any piece has a 'feel sorry for me' quality try to find at least a *moment* in which the character can rise to the occasion and honestly *challenge* their predicament. Then in the best sense of the word you will be presenting to the audience – yes – *range.*

The 'Whining and Complaining' Monologue

Just as much as you don't want to present a character who is feeling sorry for themselves you don't want to present a character who seems to always be whining and complaining. One that comes to mind is the Jennie 'I like me'speech, mentioned earlier, from Neil Simon's *Chapter Two*, nowadays on everybody's Don't Do monologue list. Long ago this speech was probably chosen by women trying to find a quick 'attention-grabber' because the character starts the speech by yelling at the person she is talking to, in this case her fiancée who can't get over grieving for his deceased first wife. The speech is problematic because the character protests too much that she is worthy and that she likes herself and yet somehow we don't really believe her. Similar to the 'Feel Sorry for Me' speech, what you can play to prevent this trap is demanding that your character fight for grace under pressure – that is, *courage* – during the speech. Your character does not have to succeed; they simply must be doing the best they can to combat an outrageous situation. They may succeed or they may fail but by golly if we see them doing the *best they can* we'll applaud for them.

The 'What a Screw-up I Am' Monologue

It may not be fair but I have heard it said that some directors and producers might get the notion *you* are the screw-up raved about in your audition monologue or song. Among classical monologues the Launce "Crab, my dog" speech from *The Two Gentlemen of Verona* is one, along with Harper from *Angels in America*, Part I and Katie from *Uncommon Women and Others*. There is a song from the musical *Seesaw* people used to do years ago for audition titled "Nobody Does It Like Me." The song does not tout the character's gifts; instead it proceeds to survey all the ways they manage to mess things up, get things wrong. Once again, if only subconsciously, over time audition watchers got the impression the person they were seeing was a screw-up *themselves!* Both this song and "Shy" from *Once upon a Mattress* rely heavily on irony, which can be difficult to depict in a very short audition. When *Mattress* first opened on Broadway they had the wonderful, over-the-top belting of Carol Burnett in her star turn to make it obvious that her character was anything *but* the thing she sang so loudly about. In sixty seconds (or thirty–forty-five if you are also doing a monologue) that is a tall order to get across to the auditors, unless you are, well, Carol Burnett. Another such song that can give an unintended impression is the whimsical "Mr. Cellophane" from *Chicago*. Now these are actually good songs; however, the hazards possible in them are instructive, especially since you can find so many others that will work better if you really can belt out a song. How about "Make Them Hear You" from *Ragtime* or "This Is the Moment" from *Jekyll and Hyde* or even "The Impossible Dream" from *Man of La Mancha*?

A good rule of thumb is to be very suspicious of a monologue in which the character is speaking badly about *themselves*.

The Dirty-Word Monologue

Unless you are auditioning for a show that contains them or are otherwise requested to provide them, you are best to avoid profane or sexually explicit language in an audition monologue. True, you are auditioning for people who at least have heard such language before (and might even use it from time to time themselves), but in the audition room you cannot be certain of the sensibilities of the auditors and it is best to avoid the possibility of offending somebody who might want to hire you. More importantly such language can become a gimmick in which you curse and swear merely for *effect*, as if to feign the danger and edge you should have had to begin with but fear you cannot display without it. Shock the auditors with your intensity as a human being who needs something from another human being, not with curse words. It may well be that one day you will perform the role of Teach in *American Buffalo* and get to speak the profanity-laced opening monologue. In the meantime – unless asked otherwise – choose to present to the auditor someone who is *talented* enough to make "Aw, Shucks!" sound as intense as if it were a more violent and foul synonym.

The 'Too Much out of Context' Monologue

Of course in choosing a monologue from a play and/or a song from a musical for audition you will be taking the material out of its written context. As it turns out, some material should never be chosen for this very reason. At an Irene Ryan Audition hosted by Kennedy Center American College Theatre Festival I once observed a couple perform the "Internet Is for Porn" song from *Avenue Q*. I might question this choice for a host of reasons but my biggest bone of contention was this: the young man playing the role of Trekkie Monster made the perfectly awful choice of attempting to replicate the gravelly 'Cookie Monster'-type voice of the character in the song. For me his work was amateurish, immature and just plain bad. Even if I had seen him do it in actual performance I would have warned him against what I considered to be a misguided decision; in the New York production the director and company understandably chose to play upon the imagined comic possibility if *Sesame Street* puppets started talking dirty. I must confess – with all due respect to folks who like this show – that this appears to be the principle appeal of the musical: the initial shock value of hearing cute puppets spouting extreme sexual language in public. As soon as the two actors began I was baffled because I had not yet seen the show. For such a prestigious scholarship competition as the Irene Ryan I would have begged the young man to pick a song from another musical he was more suitable for and likely to be cast in, such as *You're a Good Man, Charlie Brown*. My preference aside, in choosing Trekkie Monster he created a virtually insurmountable problem for himself by attempting a role that is actually meant to be a voice-over for a puppet that he does not have and we cannot see. For me all he succeeded in doing was creating dizzying confusion in the eyes of the auditors who had to wonder, as I did, "What is this kid *doing?*"

It is true that I want actors to make outrageous choices but I want them to make those choices out of their own talents, not from trying to re-do someone else's created performance.

Besides, the strident quality of the voice the young man used made me fearful of him losing his voice then and there. He was also not able to fully project or sing out because of the constriction he was causing in his throat.

To be fair, though, I have to accept that some of you out there might be tempted to try this number if you are called upon to audition with a duet someday. If you have the urge to do Trekkie Monster in an audition I would like to make a few suggestions. Just like the role you previously played onstage, re-think and re-stage the piece. Play it as if in fact you *are* the creature Trekkie Monster, right onstage in front of us, insisting on the prurient glories of the internet. That way you might be able to give us a fun show and display your comedic character talents. And also – this is vital – don't use Cookie Monster's raspy voice! Use your own focused, projected instrument so that you will be able to sing out. Who knows? Maybe you'll wind up giving us an unexpectedly fun show.

The Screenplay Monologue

I encourage you to avoid looking to film scripts to find subtle monologues for theatre. It is perfectly all right to choose these speeches for Acting-for-the-Camera class because you are learning how to act for film. Otherwise the two disciplines are almost direct opposites. A film monologue is not structured like a stage monologue; it is conceived with the understanding that a camera lens will be literally *inches* from your face. In both mediums the actor must certainly play an action to win an objective – happily that never changes – but the two styles require different tools. Film asks the actor to trust that the camera will register the moment they *think* it, which can tend to make the actor's choices small and introverted (remembering the proximity of that camera lens). Theatre asks the actor to reach out to masses of people many feet away in the same room, by *doing* it.

Speeches from screenplays are also problematic because so many are forever stamped with the famous stars that made them famous. Think of something as high-profile as Terry

Malloy's "I could'a been a contender" speech from *On the Waterfront*. No one watching this onstage is going to be able to get past the memory of Marlon Brando (that is probably why the stage version of this film has not been successful).

The One-Person-Show Monologue

Although these might be tempting, you will do well to avoid a speech that is from a one-person play. Yes they are filled with monologues – they are made up *completely* of monologues! – but that does not make them suitable for your audition. The reason is this: even though the character will have moments when they step out of the play into a 'scene' in which they must engage another invisible character, and perhaps engage them heatedly, they are still doing so less out of a need to fight for something in the here and now as much as they are *demonstrating* how their folksy, audience-pleasing character came to be the person they presented to the audience at the beginning of the evening (Like the plays *Give 'Em Hell, Harry!, Clarence Darrow, The Belle of Amherst* or *Paul Robeson*). The performer's objective, if you want to put it in that context, is to directly *please* the audience, not 'hold the mirror up to nature' in another universe. Besides, these famous one-person plays and long monologues were largely written for and performed to high acclaim by actors who were selling what *they* did best; how can you expect to breathe life into *their* material? You are YOU and must be propelled by the desire first to discover who you are and second to celebrate it to outrageous, imaginative effect during your sixty-second audition.

The Monologue You Wrote

Please avoid this vanity unless you are a published playwright whose work has stood the test of the critics and of time. Monologues we write are likely to be overly sentimental, and nearly impossible to edit; how can you possibly make cuts to your *baby*? Or worse, if they are supposed to be funny and the audience doesn't laugh …?! You may desire to use a monologue that the directors have not heard before, and that is laudable if the speech shows you off to best advantage, but your plate is full enough without having to present to them material that is more likely to hold you back than clear a path. Don't take this personally: playwrights with better skill and talent than you have toiled long and hard to generate their famous words, and those words just might get you a job someday. Trust *them.* Some organizations, such as National Unified Auditions, do not even allow original material.

The 'Big Pay-Off at the End' Monologue

You must never choose a speech for a perceived great moment at the end that is supposed to 'wow' them: the 'Big Pay-Off at the End' speech. The expectation of something wonderful happening later in the monologue always seems to cause the actor to do conspicuously *less* in the *beginning* of their performance – because they are intending to 'save themselves' for the big moment at the end. If such a moment is coming, why make us wait? Those of us who are watching have already decided what we think about you; to make us wait for your great, O. Henry-like surprise ending might be too late. Play the 'pay-off' *right from the beginning* of the speech, not at the end. Your character is constantly fighting for the right words, struggling for survival to the very last. The need to overcome an outrageous situation must drive you for the *entire* monologue, which will make your entire audition a 'pay-off.'

The Shakespeare Monologue

It is generally believed that for the sixty-second audition it is best not to attempt Shakespeare. I am inclined to agree. Still, the feisty love-for-the-Bard side of me wants to rise up and shout "Why not?"

Nine times out of ten when a theatre expressly asks for a 'classical' speech what they mean is going to be Shakespeare.

A theatre company contemplating production of a sixteenth-century play wants to hear you speak the poetry of the greatest dramatic literature of all time, and therefore they mean, when they ask for such a monologue, the works of William Shakespeare. Look closely at the casting notices; if they want Molière couplets or Greek verse they will say so. Mostly they will want to hear how you 'handle' blank verse (otherwise known as iambic pentameter). They want to hear if you can speak it in such a way that will make it sound both accessible as well as 'classic.' If it is comedic and in prose (the form that most of Shakespeare's comedic characters speak) they want to be assured that you are able to make sense of the 400-year-old slang. In other words they want to know that you can make it sound like it's your everyday speech at the same time that you have moved their heart or tickled their funny bone. Certainly there will be the occasional requests for others, like Goldsmith or Marlowe; but shouldn't you seek first from the very best?

That said, I have to admit that for the most part it is wise to avoid choosing Shakespeare for the unified sixty-second audition because doing it well honestly requires no small amount of training, and more importantly it is unlikely the companies will be casting even one Shakespeare play, let alone a season. Instead have it in your back pocket if you must, but not as the first choice. Doing homework on the theatre companies attending the auditions will help you know this. Keep the material you pick in the ballpark of show they will likely be doing so they can get a good look at how you might perform one of those roles.

The Pre-Twentieth-Century Monologue

If you are convinced that a speech from works of modern drama – such as Ibsen, Shaw, Wilde, Strindberg *et al.* – will show you off to best advantage (and even if you were I would still suggest that you could find something contemporary that would work better and do the same thing) try at least to keep them as additional monologues you might use to show variety at a callback, and strive to pick material no more challenging than the farcical one-acts of Anton Chekhov: *A Marriage Proposal* and *The Bear*, for instance. This is *if* you do them fantastically well and *if* you can find genuine humor and love in them. Also when you perform them use diction that is no more affected than clear, American *English*.

The 'Remembering the *Past*' Monologue

Don't do a monologue that is about remembering the past unless you can apply it to what you are fighting for in the here and now. These speeches are similar to some of the Williams pitfalls, in that they can cause the actor to fall in love with mood instead of the need to fight for something. Actors love to do a speech onstage where the character is looking back; they seem to jump at the chance to show the audience that they can be sentimental, and 'real' onstage. What isn't realized is that in doing such a speech the actor is essentially attempting to film-act – *onstage*. A stage play cannot pan up close to your face like a camera, gentle music playing to punctuate your gentle words – if it could it would cease to be theatre. Such pieces tend to be *inactive*. Unfortunately the great Tennessee Williams, mentioned above, is a repeat offender here. In addition to creating the hot, virile beast that is Stanley Kowalski he also created the troubled, autobiographic Tom in *The Glass Menagerie*. Don't get me wrong here; *Menagerie* is a great play and Tom a great role. It is simply that you have to be cautious with his 'Paradise Dance Hall' speech. It can become the very stuff of indulgent reminiscence: without visible action, just imagery. In such speeches as this try to do all that you can to fight against the dreamy 'looking back' quality and concentrate on what you are struggling tooth and nail to get in the here and now of the scene. In Williams' defense, Tom admits with the first lines he speaks that the play is "memory." The actor playing the role, though, should concentrate not on this non-realism as much as on Tom's maddening desire to *escape his dead-end life*.

In productions of the play I have seen this is missed in favor of being maudlin. If, however, you really want to do this speech because you are convinced that it will make you look good, try working on it from these points of view:

1. It must be about fighting for a *truth* in the *here and now.*
2. You must not give in to the temptation to *listen to your own voice.*
3. If the speech is positive, play it as a fight to *regain* those happy days!
4. If the speech is negative play it as a fight to *overcome* the same tragedy that destroyed you so long ago!

By its nature this type of monologue can be narcissistic and self-wallowing. In the same way that the audience does not need you to help them along with their feelings or prompt them to like you they also do not need for you to demonstrate how lovely or horrible your character's past was. Don't play mood – fight for an objective in an outrageous situation. As Uta Hagen said, quoting an acting teacher of hers, "Mood spelled backwards is *Doom!*" In Tom's *Menagerie* speech, for example, make it about ranting over how awful it is that those dancing, unaware young people at the Paradise Dance Hall are about to be vaporized by the bombs of war!

In Appendix A in the back of this book you will find a list of specific plays and characters in them who have monologues you might try.

Summary of "Picking Your Monologue"

1. A play is about people caught in an outrageous situation caused by love.
2. A monologue in a play is an outrageous situation.
3. In the sixty-second audition you must clearly be fighting for something.
4. Choose a monologue based on your Type, what you do best and what is age-appropriate.

5. It is best to select a comedic monologue for a unified audition.

6. If you choose a dramatic speech it will be necessary to find variety of emotion, especially humor.

7. Choose monologues from full-length published plays that can be read.

8. Do not choose monologues that require a foreign accent.

9. Avoid monologues that you wrote, that contain foul language (unless asked for), are from the internet, are from screenplays or are from Shakespeare.

10. Research the theatre companies you are auditioning for to learn if they are casting plays containing roles you can play.

Part II

WORKING ON YOUR MONOLOGUE

To business that we love we rise betime
And go to't with delight.

Antony and Cleopatra

5

GETTING STARTED

Once you have chosen the monologue you would like to use for your audition you will then rehearse it and get it ready for the big day. This is best done months in advance. Of course you will be memorizing it and making cuts if it is too long for sixty seconds. Before you get to that there will be much more for you to do in the process. I would like to suggest the following steps to get started.

Step One: Read the Play

This may be obvious but first you must read the entire play. You will do this differently from the way you study the script to play the entire role onstage. You picked the monologue to begin with because you believed that it would serve the Type you are selling, fitting both the audition itself and the theatre company or companies you are preparing for. Whether the speech you find is complete in one block or if you think you can piece together a good speech from a promising scene between characters you are scanning it for all the things you can use to convince the auditors that you have depth and imagination as well as the ability to act. So with this reading you are not trying to imagine the full arc of the role itself. Instead you are using the Given Circumstances of the play to add richness as you put together your performance.

Step Two: What Are the Given Circumstances?

Given Circumstances are everything that has happened to everyone in the play before the play begins and everything that is
understood to be true about those characters when the curtain
goes up. This of course includes the scene in which your chosen
monologue appears. What happened before is vital to the story
even though the playwright did not include all of it in complete
detail (they do it this way because otherwise the play would have
been too long). These circumstances are usually placed in the
text in the form of italicized stage directions, or talked about
in dialogue between characters early in the play; the action of
imparting this information through conversation is called *exposition*. Exposition requires great skill; the trick is to make the dialogue sound like normal conversation between characters while
at the same time presenting to the audience valuable information about what has happened before. Henrik Ibsen is particularly renowned for his ability to do this. Check out the reunion
between Nora and Mrs. Linde in the opening scene of *A Doll's
House* and you will see what I mean. Sometimes the drama-
turge might even list exposition in synopsis in the playbill. The
Given Circumstances contain everything about your character
and about all the other characters in the play deemed important: if you were rich or poor, privileged or suffered hardship;
if you are a policeman or a common thief, a businessman or
laborer; where you were born; what your family life is or was; if
you are married or divorced; if you have been lucky or unlucky
in love; and most importantly what may have gone wrong in
your life in the past. Given Circumstances also include the technical points of the town the play is set in, the time of day, year,
month and season. The playwright has chosen all of these specifically to use in the plot of the story. They are important to
you because they contain nuggets of information that can help
motivate your character's monologue in the play. This said, it
will be difficult to try to play every single particle of these circumstances, and you wouldn't do that even if you were playing

the role in performance. Survey the Given Circumstances for the *best*, most interesting character traits or events from the past that will bring your character's monologue to life. How do you do this? Some examples:

In William Inge's fine play *Picnic*, Hal Carter runs into an old college friend, Alan Seymour, in the first act. They carouse and catch up on old times. During their conversation, which seems at times innocent enough, we find out that:

- they were in a fraternity together;
- Hal went to Hollywood to become an action hero in the movies;
- Hal owes Alan money;
- Hal was robbed by two women who took his money and "had their way with him";
- Hal cut classes in school;
- Hal was a football hero in school;
- nothing like this has ever happened to Alan, etc., etc.

These are all Given Circumstances. From them the audience will get to know what Hal is like and what his relationship is to Alan as well as other people. In the early stage directions Inge refers to Hal as "exceedingly handsome," "husky," a "vagabond" and a "bum." He then supports these qualities with additional Given Circumstances unearthed in this scene. If an actor is performing a monologue of Hal's from the play it will help them create nuance in their performance if they can play actions the audience can believe of someone who is handsome, a vagabond, a guy who was a football hero and who cut class in school, among other things. How would such a person move? Gesture? Stand? Sit? Walk? Talk? Just keep in mind that these qualities provided by Inge are still qualities and *states of being*, so the actor must translate them into what he can *do* to manifest them. In this way you use the evidence of Given Circumstances to inform and shape your performance.

Step Three: "Three Tips" from the Script

In your reading of the play, along with your lines and the cues that precede them you will come across three things that will become very helpful to you as you build the motivation for your monologue. The playwright has embedded them in the play to help you. I am fond of calling them the "Three Tips from the Script." They are moments in the play when:

1. The playwright says something about *you* in the stage directions.
2. Other characters speak about *you* in their scenes.
3. *You* speak about *yourself.*

Everything that is said in one of these three instances is vital to the acting choices you might make; it is what the playwright truly thinks about you, what the other characters think about you, and what you think about yourself. These points are meant to foreshadow what your character might do later in the play, foretelling the audience *what you are capable of.* Foreshadowing is important in drama so that when your character suddenly does something unexpected the audience won't be made to shout "Where did *that* come from? That makes so little sense I am completely taken out of the reality of the play!" These Three Tips are actually more important than background Given Circumstances because they are directly linked to what you look like and what you have done and more importantly what is *said.* It is as if the author is stating "Here is how I want you to play this part. Signed, the Playwright." As a general rule of scene study for an actor it is important to assume that characters *always tell what they believe to be the truth unless the play or they themselves makes clear their reasons to lie.* That is why the actor studying a scene should pay close attention to *every word* spoken about *them.*

Think of yourself as Sherlock Holmes using deductive reasoning with the Three Tips. It might play out like this:

1. *Playwright* says about me:
   - "A squeezing, wrenching, grasping, covetous old sinner."
2. *Other characters* say about me:
   - "What right have you to be dismal? What right have you to be remorseful? You're rich enough!"
   - "Would you know the weight of the strong coil you bear yourself?"
   - "Another idol has displaced me."
   - "Poor Ebeneezer – you fear the world too much. I have seen your nobler aspirations fall, one by one, until the master passion, Gain, engrosses you."
   - "May you be happy in the life you have chosen."
3. *I* say about myself:
   - "There is nothing on which the world is as hard as poverty, and there is nothing it professes to condemn with such severity as the pursuit of wealth."
   - "I wish to be left alone. I don't make merry myself at Christmas and I can't afford to make idle people merry."
   - "If they would rather die they had better do it and decrease the surplus population."
   - "Christmas! Nothing but a poor excuse to pick a man's pocket every twenty-fifth of December."
   - "Bah! Humbug!"
4. Conclusion:
   - My possible objective(s): protect my money, keep my employee in line, defend the pursuit of wealth and jail the poor.
   - My possible action(s): to hoard, to sneer, to punish, to ridicule, to persecute, to grumble, etc.

These are just a few of the Three Tips found in the script an actor could seize upon if cast as Ebeneezer Scrooge in *A Christmas Carol*. Always look to these "Three Tips," particularly in scenes *before* your monologue appears. Sometimes the playwright will even provide tips about the characters in the cast list. Returning to the play *Picnic*, Inge describes the character Madge as "A beautiful young girl." The director will follow such indications in casting because the playwright is making clear what he wants Madge *to look like.* The actress cast as Madge can use this psychology of being 'beautiful' as she works on the role. That psychology is written into the plot, as well, for throughout the play Madge is dealing with the issue of being thought only beautiful on the outside with no substance inside. You can probably imagine the dramatic possibilities if you are playing a character who on one hand is praised for her outward beauty and on the other hand is dismissed as vapid and without substance because of it! Being at war within oneself is always an exciting acting choice, filled with potential for outrageous choices.

Step Four: Ask the Stanislavski Questions

Even though you are studying the play for its material you will still have to ask basic acting questions about motivation, like those you may have already been prompted to ask in acting class. They are of course inspired by famed Russian acting teacher Konstantin Stanislavski.

- Who are you?
- Where are you?
- Who are you talking to?
- What do you want *from them* or want to *make them do?*
- What do you *do* to accomplish this?

The first thing any acting coach will ask you is "Who are you talking to?," followed by "What do you want from them?"

The order of these questions is instructive. Plays are about *relationship and desire.* Begin with the people around you; in a monologue they are 'who you are talking to.' Next decide what your desire is – in a monologue your desire translates into 'what you want from them,' which is your objective in speaking. In order to give the auditors your best performance these questions must be answered in language that is as clear and as specific as possible. I speak about this later in the book when I address 'kind of' choices and 'kind of' acting. By 'kind of' I mean that choices are fuzzy or unspecific. This is not picky semantics. It matters *how* you describe what you want and what you are doing. It can drive impatient young actors crazy to have to be so painstaking in what can appear to be the mere selection of words, but it is not overly analytical to nail down your motivation into the form of a simple, declarative sentence. For example, which choice listed below do you think is clearest and easiest to play?

Objective/Motivation	*What you do to get it (i.e., your Action)*
I want to get to know you better	Like, try to get kind of sort of close
	Or
I must make you love me	Kiss, caress, soothe, hug

Of the choices above, which objective might you consider vague and which is stated more plainly so that you understand what is expected of you? Which Action more clearly states what you *do*? Take another look: notice the difference in the tone of the two phrase choices, "I want to" versus "*I must*." Knowing exactly what you are doing at all times is not going to make you a robot; instead this knowledge is going to be the anchor you can hang onto during an audition (in fact any performance) in which you will be nervous to begin with, no matter how good you are or how well prepared you are. That is also why it is so important to carefully study the play your chosen monologue comes from.

Step Five: Memorize!

Memorize your monologue so that you know it backwards and forwards. This means being able to speak it without thinking, over any distraction, knowing it so well that you are nearly bored by it. I'm not kidding. This will give you the freedom while doing it to act on a whim if a great idea come to you, making you more sensitive to exciting discoveries that can spark within you when you are truly 'into' it. (One quick warning about sudden 'inspirations,' however: they are best done only after you have gained considerable skill in your acting and auditioning, otherwise they can be dangerous. They are best done in rehearsal when you have time to judge whether they are appropriate or not. The outrageous you are aiming for has to be *controlled,* not chaotic.)

Never attempt to memorize your monologue the night before the audition, I promise you this will sabotage it. I have never seen this accomplish anything other than create the scenario where the actor's objective winds up being "What's my next line?!" Not being sure of your words might make for interesting acting moments in the rehearsal hall but such a hiccup during an audition will only make sure that you won't get the job.

Part of your memorization is to be very familiar with the Given Circumstances and the Three Tips from the Script. If you know exactly what is supposed to happen *before* and *after* you speak you might be able to fake your way out of the scary event of suddenly forgetting a line. It will also help you to handle a director's adjustment during a callback.

In suggesting you study the script so closely I am not trying to make a Dramatic Scholar out of you. Think of it as reaching into an arsenal for as many weapons as you can find to take into battle with you. This form of textual analysis is about the display of blood and guts onstage, not about deep thoughts and rumination. Yes, for motivation you study what happens before your character's monologue appears, but ultimately that motivation is *relative*; since you are not playing the full role in a run of the play you have free license to invent and adjust the believability necessary for the speech so that it *sells who you are better.* That is number one. The best way to insure this is to know what you are doing at all times and that is why you follow these steps and answer these questions about your monologue.

6

CUTTING AND PIECING
TOGETHER YOUR MONOLOGUE

Sometimes you will fall in love with a monologue that is long, perhaps even as long as a page. To make sure that it only runs sixty seconds you will have to make cuts to it. This is tricky but it can be done. The resulting speech should:

- have a Beginning, Middle and End;
- demand that you fight for something;
- be motivated by love or motivated by hate *because* of love.

Fig. 6.1 suggests the course your monologue wants to follow. As you can see the bubbles grow ever larger toward the *end*, meaning of course that it is here that you reach your greatest height of revelation and change as you finish the speech.

In Fig. 6.2 you can see how a speech of Cherie from William Inge's *Bus Stop* might be edited. Beginning with the top of the page to the bottom (because what I want to use is in this section) I have broken down the dialogue to be chosen for my final monologue into four parts. As much as possible, as I have tried to do, you will want to balance changes so that starting with the beginning through the end of the speech Cherie can go through a *transformation*, so that she will be different at the end of the monologue than she was at the beginning. You might build the progression like this:

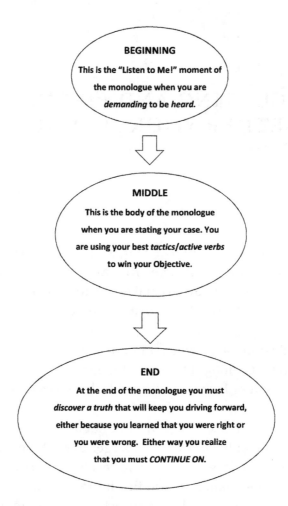

Figure 6.1 Monologue progression

- #1 – in love with/attracted to Bo;
- #2 – disappointed in/frustrated with Bo;
- #3 – resolved to leave Bo (a single line but still helpful);
- #4 – defeated by Bo and going to Montana (at the bottom of the page).

The actress is able to go through love, frustration, decision, resolve and finally to defeat in sixty seconds' time. You want

CHERIE

CHERIE   Mebbe. Anyway . . . I'd never seen a cowboy before. Oh, I'd seen 'em in movies, a course, but never in the
flesh . . . Anyway, he's so darn healthy-lookin', I don't
mind admittin', I was attracted, right from the start. #1

ELMA   You were?

CHERIE   But it was only what ya might call a *sexual* attrac-
tion.

ELMA   Oh!

CHERIE   The very next mornin', he wakes up and hollers,
"Yippee! We're gettin' married." I honestly thought he was
crazy. But when I tried to reason with him, he wouldn't
listen to a word. He stayed by my side all day long, like a
shadow. At night, a course, he had to go back to the rodeo,
but he was back to the Blue Dragon as soon as the rodeo
was over, in time fer the midnight show. If any other fella
claimed t'have a date with me, Bo'd beat him up. #2

ELMA   And you never told him you'd marry him?

CHERIE   No! He kep tellin' me all week, he and Virge'd be
by the night the rodeo ended, and they'd pick me up and
we'd all start back to Montana t'gether. I knew that if I was
around the Blue Dragon that night, that's what'd happen. #3
So I decided to beat it. One a the other girls at the Blue
Dragon lived on a farm 'cross the river in Kansas. She said
I could stay with her. So I went to the Blue Dragon last
night and just sang fer the first show. Then I told 'em I
was quittin' . . . I'd been wantin' to find another job anyway . . . and I picked up my share of the kitty . . . but
darn it, I had to go and tell 'em I was takin' the midnight
bus. They had to go and tell Bo, a course, when he come in
a li'l after eleven. He paid 'em five dollars to find out. So
I went down to the bus station and hadn't even got my
ticket, when here come Bo and Virge. He just steps up to
the ticket window and says, "Three tickets to Montana!" #4
I din know what to say. Then he dragged me onto the bus
and I been on it ever since. And somewhere deep down inside me, I gotta funny feelin' I'm gonna end up in Montana.
(*She sits now in troubled contemplation as* ELMA *resumes
her work. On the other side of the stage,* BO, *after a period
of gestation, begins to question* VIRGIL)

BO   Tell me somethin', Virge. We been t'gether since my
folks died, and I allus wondered if mebbe I din spoil yer
chances a settlin' down.

Figure 6.2 Cherie monologue from Bus Stop

such progression to be in your final cutting whether the overall mood of the speech is intimately quiet or rousingly loud.

Please remember, however, that these four progressions are the *RESULT* of the actor *playing an **action** to win an **objective***. Therefore, let me list them once more, adding possible actions to play to effect these results:

- #1 – in love with/attracted to Bo – ACTIONS: to purr, giggle, flutter, worship, adore;
- #2 – disappointed in/frustrated with Bo – ACTIONS: to complain, grouse, moan, bitch;
- #3 – resolved to leave Bo – ACTIONS: to surrender, bow, frown, pout, whine;
- #4 – defeated by Bo – ACTIONS: to mope, rail, lash out, murmur.

Always remember that the movement of your performance has to be broken down in terms of what you can DO.

Piecing Together a Monologue from a Longer Scene

Sometimes you search and search and you cannot seem to find a monologue that dazzles you. Then suddenly you come across a scene in a play that is fun, exciting, and you are moved to think "If *only ...!*" Here you might be able to 'piece together' a monologue – that is, take all of the *response* lines of the character you want to play and combine them into a *single speech*, adding in crucial cues from the other character if necessary to bridge transitions. When performing the speech you play these add-ins as if your character were asking a question of *themselves* out loud for which they already know the answer.

This will take a little time and concentration. In a way you are putting yourself into the position of the playwright and trying to construct a sixty-second speech that has all of the dramatic dynamics of a good monologue.

The character Bill Starbuck in *The Rainmaker* by N. Richard Nash has several fine monologues an actor can use to display fire,

LIZZIE. No!

STARBUCK. I'll ask it anyway. Why are you fussin' at the buttons on your dress?

LIZZIE. Fussing at the—! I'm not! *(And she stops doing it.)*

STARBUCK. *(Evenly, gently)* Let 'em alone. They're all buttoned up fine. *(Circles to Left of her.)* As tight as they'll ever get— And it's a nice dress too. Brand new, ain't it? You expectin' somebody?

LIZZIE. None of your business.

STARBUCK. A woman gets all decked out—she must be expectin' her beau. Where is he? —it's gettin' kinda late.

LIZZIE. *(Breaking out)* I'm not expecting anybody! *(To Center.)*

STARBUCK. *(Quietly)* Oh I see. You were—but now you ain't. Stand you up?

LIZZIE. Mr. Starbuck, you've got more gall—! *(And she starts for the stairs. But he grabs her arm.)*

STARBUCK. Wait a minute!

LIZZIE. Let go of me!

STARBUCK. *(Tensely)* The question I really wanted to ask you before—it didn't have nothin' to do with buttons! It's this: The minute I walked into your house— you didn't like me! Why?!

LIZZIE. I said let go!

STARBUCK. *(Letting her go)* You didn't like me—why? Why'd you go up on your hind legs like a frightened mare?!

LIZZIE. I wasn't frightened, Mr. Starbuck! You paraded yourself in here—and you took over everything! I don't like to be taken by a con man!

STARBUCK. *(Lashing out)* Wait a minute! I'm sick and tired of this! I'm tired of you queerin' my work, callin' me out of my name!   #1

LIZZIE. I called you what you are—a big-mouthed liar and a fake!

STARBUCK. *(With mounting intensity)* How do you know I'm a liar? How do you know I'm a fake? Maybe I *can* bring rain! Maybe when I was born God whis-   #2

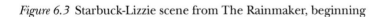

Figure 6.3 Starbuck-Lizzie scene from The Rainmaker, beginning

pered a special word in my ear! Maybe He said: "Bill
Starbuck, you ain't gonna have much in this world! You
ain't gonna have no wife and no kids—no green little
house to come home to! But Bill Starbuck—wherever
you go—you'll bring rain!" Maybe that's my one and
only blessing!

#3

LIZZIE. *(To Left of sofa.)* There's no such blessing in
the world!

STARBUCK. *(Center.)* I seen even *better* blessings,
Lizzie-girl! I got a brother who's a doctor. You don't
have to tell him where you ache or where you pain! He
just comes in and lays his hand on your heart and pretty
soon you're breathin' sweet again! And I got another
brother who can sing—and when he's singin', that song
is *there!*—and never leaves you! *(With an outcry)* I
used to think—why ain't *I* blessed like Fred or Arny?

#4

Why am I just a nothin' man, with nothin' special to my
name? And then one summer comes the drought—and
Fred can't *heal* it away and Arny can't *sing* it away! But
me—I go down to the hollow and I look up and I say:
"Rain! Dammit!—*please!*—bring rain!" And the rain
came! And I knew—I knew I was one of the family!

#5

(She sits, Left end of sofa.)
(Suddenly quiet, angry with himself.) That's a story.
You don't have to believe it if you don't want to. *(He
sits, Right end of sofa.)*

LIZZIE. *(A moment. She is affected by the story—but
she won't let herself be. She pulls herself together with
some effort.)* I *don't* believe it!

STARBUCK. You're like Noah! You don't believe in
anything!

LIZZIE. That's not true!

STARBUCK. Yes it is! You're scared to believe in anything! You put the fancy dress on—and the beau don't
come! So you're scared that *nothin'll ever come!* You got
no faith!

LIZZIE. *(Crying out)* I've got as much as anyone!

STARBUCK. You don't even know what faith is! And
I'm gonna tell you! It's believin' you see white when

Figure 6.4 Starbuck-Lizzie Scene from The Rainmaker, continued

bombast and good humor, all at the same time. I have included it here because I have used it myself for audition. It can be very theatrical and yet there are opportunities for simple honesty as well. The speech is in the middle of Act II, and the scene is between Starbuck and Lizzie Curry. Using the text of the Samuel French Acting Edition, pages 50 and 51, you can see that the scene is spread over these pages. On page 50 Starbuck is finally fed up and angrily tells Lizzie so, challenging her because she has been so hard on him. This is the body of the speech you will want to work on. Editing it is actually very simple. Lizzie has only one response that interrupts Starbuck's speech, which can easily be taken out. What you have left is what you will work on – remembering that you will still need to do further cutting so that it fits into the sixty-second time limit. The real challenge will probably come from deciding which of his great fun lines to take out. In going through the editing process it will help to think about the way people actually argue, which I mention in a moment.

Once you have the cutting you like, speak it out loud for timing to make sure that it runs only sixty seconds or a little less. Remember:

1. The final pieced-together speech has a clear beginning, middle and end.
2. With the beginning you are *demanding* to be heard.
3. With the middle you are *stating* your case to win your objective.
4. With the end you *discover or resolve the truth.*
5. Cut redundant lines; characters in a contentious scene often repeat themselves out of angst. These repeats can go, especially in a sixty-second monologue; you only need to make a clear point once or twice at the most.

The monologue progression in the Starbuck monologue might be tracked like this, with actions listed here in **bold**:

#1 – Starbuck **blows up** with Lizzie.
#2 – Starbuck **demands** to know why Lizzie distrusts him.

#3 – Starbuck **assures** Lizzie that he has been blessed.
#4 – Starbuck **shares** with Lizzie the blessings in his family.
#5 – Starbuck **celebrates** the fact that he has been blessed.

Think of numbers 1–5 as 'beats' – units of action – which change as your character goes through their monologue. Also notice that in each number Starbuck performs an active verb (blows up, demands, assures, etc.). You can number your individual cuts as you choose. I have tried this cutting out loud for myself and it does indeed run sixty seconds, so you are going to be pleasantly surprised by how much acting you can do in that short a time.

Sometimes you might decide to piece together a monologue and include some of the responses from the other character, and incorporate them into your speech as your own character's dialogue. Consider Sid and Flo in Scene III, "The Young Hack and His Girl," from Clifford Odets' depression-era play *Waiting for Lefty*. Sid has arrived at Flo's apartment to pick her up for a date. They exchange pleasantries and then the conversation gets serious. Flo's family is not happy with the fact that she and Sid have been "engaged" for three years, and there is no prospect for them to ever get married. Sid is a hard-working cab driver who cannot get ahead because of the "bigshot money men" who are stacking the deck against hard-working people like himself – the play is an outcry for the burgeoning union movement in the United States – and because of this they can never afford to have a life together, let alone have kids, which would be a big part of their impossible marriage.

In this potential cutting, which you will find on page 20 in *Waiting for Lefty and Other Plays*, published by Grove Press, you can take two lines from Flo and give them to Sid. This enables him to lament about wanting to have kids and realizing that outside forces keep them scrounging around, and this can finally motivate his growing anger about the powers of big business and how the little people would rise up and fight if only they had the chance.

You might break down the dramatic progression/beats like this:

- BEMOANING the fact that he won't be able to have a family with Flo;
- BOASTING of his love for Flo;
- MOURNING over the outside forces that keep them lonely;
- ATTACKING with a threat directed toward the "money men";
- GIVING UP finally in confessing that he is at a loss for words.

Once again, each of these beats during the speech is listed as an *active verb*, which keeps the actor *doing* rather than *feeling*. Feeling is certainly at the heart of what plays are about but the performer must concentrate only on what is within their control – playing an action to get an objective and allowing the emotion to take care of itself. With choices such as these the actor is able to depict emotions ranging from sadness to happiness to anger to sadness again, providing a complexity of human need so that the monologue is not performed with only one intention.

And I did test the cutting to make sure that it fits in the sixty-second run time.

For actors trying to find the best active verb I recommend an excellent book, *Actions: The Actor's Thesaurus*, by Marina Calderone and Maggie Lloyd-Williams. It is a wonderful, comprehensive A-to-Z reference with Emotional Groupings to help you find what you are looking for much faster. You can order it from the website, http://actionsforactors.com/, and as you might guess it is also now available as an app on iPhone, iPad and iPod Touch.

7

GET ON YOUR FEET

Put together very simple staging for your monologue. This will include your entrance and your exit, both of which you will rehearse. If you choose to use a chair – see my note about it below – move it into place before you announce your name, number and audition package.

Blocking and How to Move (Because You *Must* Move)

Substantively, with blocking – which is motivation *with movement* – you will first establish a 'performance' space for yourself onstage. This can be done by drawing an imaginary circle all around yourself stage *center*, about four or five feet on all four sides of you. In Fig. 7.1 you can get an idea. Think of this as your 'playing area.' As you rehearse and perform your monologue, remain in this circle. It will keep you from wandering too far left or right and enable you to remain fundamentally center. It will also help you to avoid making the mistake some actors do of inching so far downstage they are nearly out of the light and come perilously close to falling off the edge of the stage. If you find that you are wandering this means you are not clear on your objective and action and even where your character physically is in the scene, so you will need to make it clear for yourself.

Place the imaginary listener out in front of you, center. This is if you are speaking to a single person. If by chance you are

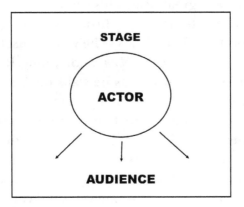

Figure 7.1 Audition-playing area onstage

speaking to more than one person – for instance if your character is addressing a jury – make the 'room' by placing a specific
imaginary person left and right as well as center. This will help
us to 'see' the jury as well as the 'room.' If you are speaking to
two separate people, place each of them downstage of you, at
slight left and right angles to you. This will prevent you from
giving too much profile to the auditors and it will give you a
specific target on which to fix your gaze. For speeches spoken
alone establish your focus out front, center. If you are in a small
rehearsal hall-type room you can stay focused center, simply
directing your speech just over the heads of the auditors sitting
in the rows of seats or at the table or you can place your focus at
an immediate diagonal as long as you guard against too much
profile. In the heat of your performance you are certainly free
to look from left to right as well as center, acting and reacting,
as long as you are not pulled out of your 'playing area.'

Depending on the monologue you have chosen it may be that
you will wind up moving very little. Many audition speeches,
especially when the actions are clear, tend to settle and hold
center because characters are most likely confronting someone
head-on, directly, whether out of animus or love. Others, however, that are just as focused and action-driven might require

the actor to move a great deal. This can happen with speeches in which the character is in the throes of either great turmoil or great celebration (Benedick's "The world must be peopled!" speech from *Much Ado about Nothing* or young Richard going through emotional confusion as he waits for his girlfriend on the dune in *Ah! Wilderness*). The important thing is to think of movement as coming out of great need, either to send the other character a message or if alone to plead aloud for a solution.

Even though you will want to move at least a little just to move, don't do it too much. I know this may sound confusing but it is actually about motivation. Movement should come organically out of the action in the speech; for instance in an angry huff in the middle of an argument you might take a step or two in one direction as if to get away and then realize that you want to say more and so you decide to come back: movement that is script- as well as need-based. Construct and rehearse any movement in your monologue the same way you would if you were blocking the scene in the play. It *is* blocking.

Give careful thought to whether you will get down on the floor. If you do, remember that you will have to *get back up*. There is an exercise related to this in Chapter 8, "Exercises to Get Outrageous." I have gone back and forth with this idea over the years, and most recently I have come down on the side of the outrageous. I used to prefer that if you got down onto the floor it would work best if you did so during the *middle* of the monologue so that you had the rest of the scene to get back to your feet gracefully. But I forgot – silly me! – that the risk of clumsiness and looking stupid was only something the *performer* should avoid, *not* the *character*. Your character shouldn't give a darn if they might look clumsy or stupid; they are too busy trying to deal with an outrageous situation! Clumsiness and stupidity are forgiven of fallible human beings. The auditors aren't going to mind when you rise up from the floor to say your final "Thank you!" because they have just seen you raise the stakes in playing an action to win an objective!

Whatever choices you decide on in moving try to insure that:

1. the move is definite and committed without any hesitation;
2. through your action the audience is able to believe – at least *possibly* – the move happened because of the outrageous situation your character found themselves in;
3. Or, if *not* believable, the move is so risky and outlandish and daring – *and committed to* – that you can be given credit for your fearlessness.

By fully committing to daring choices you may force the auditor to think "Bravo! I don't agree with the choice, but I have to hand it to them for not being afraid to try it!" Just make sure that you perfect them in rehearsal first. Then it can become a great recipe for making yourself memorable.

Body Language

In Chapter 10, "And Don't Forget …," I speak about what I call "Up Good, Down Bad." This has to do with actors allowing their bodies to do things that send the wrong message about them to the auditors. In addition to establishing appropriate, unobtrusive movement/blocking to your speech you don't want to do physically what will undercut the needs of your monologue emotionally. You may have seen what I mean: an actor rants about how angry and upset their character is and yet their body is virtually immobile, does *not move an inch*, not even the raising of arms. Or they go on and on about calmness and serenity while their body is shaking like a leaf. Perhaps the most common mistake is habitually looking *down* for no good reason. These miscues are almost always done without your being aware of them; so in rehearsal have your acting teacher check to see if they creep in. They can then help you address them.

Don't Use a Chair

I recommend not using a chair. Although 99 percent of the time there will be a chair available to you in the audition room, I think a chair is a crutch that won't add to your audition and might even take interest away. The only use I have seen chairs put to is for a perceived moment in the monologue when the actor has decided that a character wants to suddenly jump up out of it, as if to dramatically react to something. Why not react dramatically while already standing? To do the other gives much more power to the chair than you want the chair to have; the scene, in effect, becomes *about the chair*.

Sitting down tends to close off your ribcage and diaphragm; the very act of sitting is a retiring energy that suggests *retreat from* versus a *drive toward*. For sixty seconds you are fighting for your life, not settling down to take a rest.

Don't Mime

If your audition monologue requires the use of props ditch it and find another. The same thing is true of mime. Even if you were Marcel Marceau (the most famous mime who ever lived) you would not serve yourself in miming objects. The speech is about you and your needs, not about demonstrating how well you can replicate objects that are not there. There is even the danger that you might give the auditor the impression that you were more suitable to perform on the streets of Central Park than in their theatre company. Actually I'm kidding about that. What I mean is never mime anything that the character must *actually have*; then the speech becomes about how well (or how poorly) you mime it. If the character must mime, reduce the activity to the gestures a person speaking would make when describing something they *know* they do not have in their hands, such as finger-pointing, or when people crook their fingers and thumb to their ears to suggest a telephone receiver. Doing it this way you are clearly not attempting to indicate anything other than what your need is in speaking.

Just the same a speech requiring that much attention to pantomime is probably not a good pick anyway. You are not auditioning for a mime troupe; you are trying to 'hold the mirror up to nature' using your body to depict the entire canon of dramatic literature!

Beginning, Middle and End

Your audition presentation must have the same dynamics your monologue must have, in that it too should be presented in the form that contains a beginning, middle and end. In this regard you may truly look on your audition as telling a story, a mini-play in which you have taken the auditors on a voyage and then returned them back to their seats safe and sound when you finally say "Thank you."

Beginning

Your audition begins as soon as you enter the room. This is the *actor* portion of the speech; the *character* portion begins the nanosecond following your introduction. At this point you have built into your speech the *need to speak*.

1. Rehearse what your imaginary scene partner has *just* said that demands a reply.
2. If alone, play what has *just* driven you into the room.
3. Your first words are *demands to listen*; this is true if you are speaking to someone or if you are speaking aloud when alone. In the same way that you shout "HOLD IT!" or "TIME OUT!" to get attention in a heated argument this is what the beginning of your monologue must fundamentally do and be about.

Note: as you begin your monologue you obviously do not necessarily always need to shout. It is necessary for you to speak with the urgency that a desire to get attention demands. The very first objective of your character is to *make them listen to you*.

Middle

The middle of your monologue is when you truly fight for what you want. This is where you 'make your case.'

• During the middle of the speech you are constantly making *discoveries* that will drive you to greater heights, either because you are winning or because you are losing. Arguments go on and on because people remember *grievances* that caused them to need to speak up in the first place, or they decide to *celebrate* the fact that they got in some good jabs at their adversary and want to rub their adversary's nose in it – the "and *ANOTHER* thing!" moment. This will also keep you changing tactics, which will prevent you from playing the speech only one way. Always making a *new* discovery helps the monologue to 'play' by keeping it energized and in the moment, and most importantly it compels the character to *change*.

End

You have stated your case, you have fought for what you wanted, propelled by constant self-discovery along the way. Perhaps you are exhausted – in any case you are enervated by such strenuous human endeavor. Upon completing the journey you have just taken us on there is still a moment for one last capper, a final punctuation to celebrate a job well done; with your exit from the room you are nearly teasing them with the expectation of what might be possible for them if they are smart enough to call you back! This is the final piece of your audition and you don't want to give it short shrift. Rehearse it just as much as your entrance and introduction. It is about convincing the auditors how professional you are as well as how nice a person you are (that is, a person who won't cause problems in their theatre company). Say "Thank you" with as much courtesy as your introduction, and try not to rush, though of course at this moment depending upon how the timing of your sixty-second audition went it is possible that you might feel hurried. Just the same, take a breath and bring your body back to center. What I mean by this is *clearly break* the theatrical reality established by the audition performance and stand with hands relaxed loosely at your sides. You are back to center by the time you finish whether it is physically 'center' or not. At the unified cattle call you will probably need to repeat your name and number. Then you will turn and leave the stage just as calmly, without rushing. The back you present to them as you exit is just as much a part of the interview – and an audition *is* an interview – so you want to avoid giving the impression that you can't wait to get out of their presence.

What Your Audition Must Be About

You have prepared your monologue for the audition. Double-check to make sure that rehearsal has included everything your performance needs to do. Make certain that with your work you convince the auditors that your audition is about:

1. Fighting for Something

As I said earlier this is the one thing that plagues the audition of young actors more than anything else. Directors watching your audition want to see you in as close to a finished performance as can be managed within the ridiculous confines of an audition stage, and the best way to get there within the actor's control is to play a character who is clearly *fighting for something*.

Monologues happen at critical moments in a play; they are never casual, no matter how quiet or intimate the scene they are delivered in might seem to be, and they are driven by deep-seated human desire in the heart of the speaker. Suppose your character does not get what they want from having spoken a monologue: would it mean their death? Or someone *else's* death?

Try this trick: ask yourself "Can the play exist *without* this speech being spoken?" If the answer to this question is "yes" then it is of no dramatic use to you and another monologue must be chosen as quickly as possible.

2. Opposites

Seek out and play the opposites in your monologue. This is similar to Shakespeare's use of *antithesis*, a rhetorical technique in which two conflicting ideas are juxtaposed against one another. Shakespeare uses it constantly in his plays to enhance the understanding of his characters by giving the audience something to compare an idea with. Whether it was intentional or not I find that the use of antithesis can help to create characters of greater depth and humanity. By balancing imagery between opposites – hot and cold, white and black, day and night, etc. – the audience is able to see characters not so far removed from themselves because they too did not have all the answers, they questioned their very existence and often weren't sure of what they could hold onto as absolute truth because there *was no* absolute truth.

I am not trying to get into a scholarly discourse on what Shakespeare actually meant with his use of antithesis. I'm talking about *flesh-and-blood human beings who mess up and don't know why.* This is what drives audition monologues – what makes you *need to speak* monologues. When the playwright has characters make these comparisons out loud in the text you can bet it is because they are pleading for an answer *outside* of themselves that has troubled them for a long time. Have you ever left someone after yelling at them, saying "Why did I do that? That's not like me!"? We flawed race of people are constantly doing the opposite of what we intend to do, going against what we proclaim ourselves assured of, breaking even our own code of right and wrong, baffling our very selves by our own actions.

As I have also said, actors should never play their monologue on only one level: either all angry or all happy. Find moments, however brief, of both. In fact, *make up* the comparisons even if they are not there! To accomplish this all you need to know is the difference between Protagonist (the person the play is about) and Antagonist (the person or forces that stand in the Protagonist's way of getting what they want). Then examples will come more easily to you: the most vicious character desires to be the most beloved, the most beloved character has moments of bitter animosity, the most clownish fool experiences depths of dark reality. Why? Because they are *human!* Your ability to create this complexity in your acting will impress whoever sees you. Can you name Shakespeare's most famous use of antithesis?

To be, or *Not* to Be, of course.

3. *You at Your Best*

The most powerful element of your audition is who you are and what you uniquely bring to the table. The late former Managing Director of the long-gone Off Broadway Equity Library Theatre (ELT), George Wojtasik, always used to speak about the showcasing of actors by telling them the company was dedicated to getting them "Looking Good." He was referring to ELT doing all that it could to provide production values – costumes, sets, lights, direction, etc. – that would help actors present their talent in the greatest possible light to agents and casting directors who came to the showcase productions. The individual actor can do this themselves. Specifically, you can present yourself at your best through:

- enjoyment in being there;
- grooming and clothing;
- courtesy and gratitude to the auditors;
- choosing material that is best suited to your Type;
- choosing material that is best suited for the majority of plays the participating theatres will be producing;
- making choices that are based on a human being doing the best they can in an outrageous situation.

As far as the performance itself is concerned, you are at your best when, at the heart of whatever speech you are doing, comedic or tragic, we see – or at least we can *believe* that we see – an actual human being struggling against the odds life has placed in front of them. Actors sometimes make the mistake of trying to replicate the performances of other admired actors instead of looking deep within themselves, or worse, they get the misguided notion that it is possible for them to *hide* behind the character, to 'become' someone else. In the space of sixty seconds you can give the auditors a glimpse of who you really are by accepting who you are, with a healthy self-love and respect for all. In other words, by doing unto others as you would have them do unto you. It is has never been said better than that. This will set you apart from other actors and allow you to give the performance that only *you* can give. It might sound corny, but truly, truly, consider every play – and every performance – as being about *love*.

4. Love

Every play, in one way or another, is about *love*. Love lost, found, wanted, requited, refused, spurned, gained, missed, longed-for and countless other iterations of human frailty in between. For the actor trying to find the outrageous in their work it is also going to be necessary to find this most universal of all human needs in the heart of their character. Even in what seems to be the dreariest role, try to find in that character something that is positive and redeemable, something that can be *loved*. Find someone or some*thing* for them *to* love. No matter how bleak or hopeless the play may appear – I can think of Shakespeare's *Timon of Athens*, in which the hero vows to shun all mankind – keep looking. Keep digging. Love has so much size that it can reach past the edge of the stage into the heart of an audience. Even in monologues driven by anger, such animus has at its core some longing for human love. Your character might be shouting to get our attention; allow that shouting to be because you love us – that is, you love the person *you are talking to or about*. If the speech is at all worth doing you will find it, and at that moment – mark my words – your performance will really start to click.

8

EXERCISES TO GET OUTRAGEOUS

You have begun to rehearse your monologue. How 'outrageous' is it? Ask yourself these questions to try to find out:

1. Would the person (or roomful of people) you are speaking to be embarrassed, either for you or themselves, while listening to it? I am not talking about you embarrassing the auditors; that is a definite no-no. Might your *imaginary* scene partner(s) be embarrassed because of something you say or are doing?
2. Are you being too personal?
3. Are you being unfair to them?
4. Are you asking too much of them?
5. Are you forced to speak against your will?
6. Are you speaking out of *love*?

These questions have nothing to do with right and wrong, especially the question of whether *you* are right or wrong. They have to do with what you are *doing* and how desperately you need to *do* it. Human need in the throes of an outrageous situation knows no boundaries, no protocol and no limits; if you are forced to steal food because you are on the streets starving to death are you going to care one whit if society believes it is wrong to steal? If your very life depended upon you saying what you are about to say in a monologue, why in the world would you care if in saying it you hurt anybody's feelings?

The outrageous situation does not end with the speaking of your monologue. To use the war metaphor, the monologue is only the weapon you have been forced to use to combat your problem in the heat of battle – the 'battle' being the play your character is in. We don't know how it will all end until the end of the play. Your forced speech is only the beginning, an opening salvo you have made not because you wanted to but because you *had* to.

Actions

By now you are probably wondering what you can actually do to make your audition monologue more 'outrageous.' Here is a brief list of wild tasks to use when rehearsing your speech. While speaking aloud inject one (or more) of these actions, all the while delivering the monologue as 'normally' as before. Just stick them in, suddenly, without regard for whether they are appropriate or not. Play with them, even make up some of your own. You never know what might happen in the rehearsal process, which of course has no such thing as right or wrong.

FALL TO YOUR KNEES	TALK BABY TALK
SCRATCH AN IMAGINARY ITCH	DO A CARTWHEEL
HAVE TO PEE	HOWL LIKE A DOG
HAVE TO ITCH	RUN FOR COVER FROM BOMBS
DO A PHONEY BRITISH ACCENT	FLY LIKE A PLANE
DO BABY TALK	DO A PIROUETTE
LAUGH OUT LOUD	MEOW LIKE A CAT
CRY PHONEY TEARS	SWIM ACROSS THE FLOOR
DANCE IN A JIG	"ARGH!" LIKE A PIRATE
WAIL ON A VOWEL	WHINE LIKE A CHILD
MAKE A KISSING SOUND	SNAKE ACROSS THE FLOOR

For Monologues that Are Dramatic ...

Play them as the biggest JOKE you ever heard.
Play them while laughing.
Play them while standing on your head.
Play them toward the ceiling while on your back on the floor.
Play them on your stomach crawling across the floor.
Play them while rolling on the floor.

Play them while running up and down the hallway.

Play them while dancing.

Play them while shadow-boxing and shout "Pow!" after every line.

Play them like a song and sing every line.

For Monologues that Are Comedic ...

Play them as the saddest TRAGEDY you ever experienced.

Play them as Melodrama.

Play them while crying.

Play them as a Murder Suspect Confession.

Play them as a Death Bed Confession.

Play them as a Preacher Delivering a Eulogy.

Play them while digging a grave.

Play them and inject "So there!" after every line.

Play them and inject a curse word after every line.

Play them as if you are under heavy artillery fire in war.

In fact do every single thing that comes to your mind to do, especially if it seems that you would *never* do such a thing.

You don't have to think about the logic of these actions. You only have to *do* them. As a matter of fact, taking the time to think about the logic of these actions is only going to result in no actions being taken at all. Don't be concerned if some of these efforts are wrong and out of place for your speech. *People in outrageous situations DO what is wrong and out of place.* Experiment with them and then ask yourself: What does such a crazy, sudden act *do* to the speech? How does it affect the object-ive? Action? Beats? *You?* Is it *possible* that such a thing could believably be worked into the body of the speech? *Is it?* Or does it stretch the bounds of believability too far for comfort?

These exercises might not work for your speech; they might in fact turn out to be inappropriate for the material. If you let them, though, they might kindle a spark in your *own* imagina-tion so that you can create more appropriate action, just as outrageous, that fits the material you are working on. That is the real benefit that is possible with these wild actions. They can help you get closer to your own material.

There is another reason, just as important, to try these wild actions during your monologue rehearsal. In addition to directing you toward interpretations that are exciting and new they will also prevent the speech from being played with only one action. Monologues done on only one level do not serve you because they do not show the auditor your range and therefore your ability to be cast. These crazy actions are meant to at least enliven the monologue and might even ignite the occasional humdrum speeches in which you might have thought "nothing is going on," leading you toward greater opposites, greater *antithesis*, so valuable in making an impact in a sixty-second monologue.

Exercises

These exercises for your monologue will work best if you have already memorized your speech and have at least a basic understanding of what your character wants. If you do not, go ahead and try them anyway. It is through trial and error that the best objectives and actions for your monologue are going to be found, after examining choice after choice, discarding one after another in favor of still another. These exercises only ask that you take your monologue wildly out of context and well past the meaning that you have already established. That is okay. They are meant as part of the process you go through toward greater freedom with your speech, which will in turn open you up to richer, more exciting choices in the life of your character. As with any improvisation the benefit comes from just jumping in and *doing it*. Discoveries will be made along the way as well as after the fact.

Exercise #1: Every Line Is a New Discovery

This simple little improvisation is designed to help the actor remember how active and immediate their desire is to fight for truth in a monologue. Try this.

- Stand and speak the speech out loud.
- Play the beginning of every new line as a *new discovery*, not thought of before.
- Then play every new discovery with a new *reaction*.
- With every new line and new discovery walk in a completely new *direction*.
- As you draw near the end of the speech allow your voice to rise in pitch and your moves to lift you off your feet; that is, hop or jump or lunge.
- Do the speech again, *immediately*, without the movement, keeping the continuing discovery.

Exercise #2: Rooting for 'Gold'

Get down on your hands and knees and start your speech.

- Begin, like a dog, to root on the floor as if you are digging with your bare hands.
- As you continue 'digging,' clamor from left to center to right, and root harder, fiercer.
- The idea is that you are feverishly digging in the earth beneath you for gold – or *something* precious – and that you are not able to find it. Allow your search to become more desperate, more impatient, letting it frustrate you to the point of being angry; where the devil *is* that thing I am looking for?!
- Be aware of your voice and reading of the monologue, allowing yourself as you go along to be affected by your violent digging; let your pitch build, words elongate, etc.
- Play it two different ways: one resulting in your *finding* what you were looking for and another in which you *fail* to find it.
- At the end of your speech let your celebration – or lament – be sung on a long, vocal wail.

Exercise #3: Make Them Believe You!

As you begin your monologue, throw in the following phrases: "Really!" "Honest!" "No, I'm not kidding!" "I'm NOT LYING!" "For REAL!" Do this constantly during the speech, after just about every line, as if the made-up dialogue were part of the written monologue. Better yet, have either your teacher or a friend constantly interrupt you with negative words, such as "I don't believe you!" "No, I don't!" "Stop lying!" "No way!" "Get out of here!" See how it drives the speech, how it causes you to nearly overlap yourself, how it causes you to pick up your own cues without rushing because you are not artificially speeding up; you are actually fighting to make yourself *understood and believed.* Then do the speech without the added words, continuing to fight to be believed, to convince the audience that you are telling the *truth*, even and especially if it is in fact a bald-faced lie!

Exercise #4: "Vowel thru" Your Monologue

In the same way that you run lines to learn your speech, go through your entire monologue mouthing out loud every vowel sound you come to. Where there are no vowels instead hit the consonants, very hard. You might sound as if you are singing a tune:

"*OooooooaaaaaaooooooooaaffffDDDDDDDoo-oonnnnnnnnoooooooaaaa!*"

In the same way that you run lines to insure that you know them word for word this exercise will take you through the movement of the monologue: the hills, the valleys, the rise and fall of the speech. Take notice of the quick, staccato sound of the consonants in comparison to the smooth, long, legato sound of the vowels. Vowels can be soothing, consoling and reassuring; consonants can be harsh and sudden, hammering in uncertainty or attack. We speak certain words with certain emphasis based on our needs and the outrageous situation we find ourselves in. For example: you bang your toe against a door. The inevitable expletive that ensues has much more power, more bang for your buck, as it were, if you hit these consonants very hard, doesn't it? Or if you smell something that is excruciatingly foul to the nose, the way you draw out the vowels

"Eeeeeeyyyyyoooooooooo!" is going to help you express your revulsion more fully, isn't it?

Exercise #5: Shout, Then Whisper

During the course of the speech find a place – planned, unplanned – where you can SHOUT a line to top of your voice. Just ONE line. Do the monologue several times this way. Then, do the speech again, without the shout, instead this time finding a spot where you can WHISPER a single line. In both cases you only choose a single line or, better yet, a single word. This can immediately give the speech emphasis and create new under-standing of the word. Sometimes it can highlight a meaning previously not realized. One such example is when I have done this exercise with students working on a monologue of Little Bit from Paula Vogel's *How I Learned to Drive.* She is challenging Uncle Peck for molesting her and at one point she mentions her age at the time it was going on. I suggested to the actress that she might, then, try shouting the single word *"Twelve!"* to the top of her voice. Just that one word. It was amazing to see how much impact such an exercise had so quickly. More than once when the actress did this the sensual meaning, the pri-mal understanding and implication of this one word – when it was understood that a minor had been sexually molested by a grown man – would result in the actress becoming emotional and even on the verge of real tears, accepting as if for the first time the true import of what Little Bit was saying.

After the fact there is always the energy of *coming down* from having just blown up. This is the premise of what happens when the character consciously tries to get control of themselves; in order to control yourself you must first *lose* control.

Exercise #6: Sing, Then Ha!

In this exercise you find a single line in your monologue – pref-erably with a period at the end of it – that you can *sing out loud.* A variation on this is for you to find a spot where your character

might interrupt themselves by shouting "HA!" Do not be concerned how sudden and out of place these improvs are; this
is only an exercise to get in touch further with how human
and unpredictable we creatures can be. We cry when we are
happy and we laugh when we are sad. Because it is, at least
on the face of it, out of place and over the top, after doing it
try to sense how this has affected the speech, how it may have
invigorated it; might your character *actually* sing a line like a
jingle at a particularly inopportune moment? Might they? After
the "HA!" see if this has driven home a certain line or point
before it: say, if Willy Loman were to blurt "I'm not a dime a
dozen! HA! I'm Willy Loman, and you're Biff Loman!" Does
not shouting "HA!" before a line tend to suggest braggadocio
on the part of the speaker? A sense of being wildly puffed up,
confident whether they are actually in such a position of power
or not? Or, conversely, if the character is consciously putting
themselves down, suddenly shouting "HA!" can suggest giving
up, a certain pessimism about their prospects, not a retreat-
ing pessimism as much as an outgoing, grandiose, *narcissistic*
pessimism. Every character in every play, no matter how bombastic or how shy (whether the heroic title character in *Cyrano
de Bergerac* or the put-upon housewife Lola in *Come Back, Little
Sheba*) is an ego maniac! At once, after injecting "HA!" do the
speech 'normally,' without adding "HA!" I am not encouraging
you to add words into famous dialogue that can stand by itself.
I just want you to see what doing this in rehearsal does to you.

Exercise #7: Hit the Deck!

This is a particularly challenging exercise, and one that I came
up with only recently. I spoke about it earlier. Up to now I have
always felt that during the course of a monologue – especially
one for people who are going to presumably hire you – you
wanted to avoid getting down on the floor. I always felt that
there was just too much possibility of causing your movement
to appear clumsy or ungraceful. Then I felt that if the actor
has decided to get down on the floor, to sit or on all fours or

whatever, they are best to do it in the middle of the speech so that they can then more or less organically build a graceful rise to their feet by speech's end.

I now see that I was wrong.

I now realize that the actor getting onto the floor ought to do it *whenever they feel like it*, as long as they can make it the result of an outrageous situation caused by love. As long as your skill has risen to the power to perform it, auditioning requires the willingness to risk.

For this exercise the actor – as in the case of all of the other exercises – is asked to just do it – during their monologue, drop down to the floor. Just like that. Fall! Splat! Then they continue the speech and see what happens. See how you *rise up*; are you slow, fast, clumsy, graceful, confused, embarrassed, dusting yourself off, etc? What does such a violent act do to your speech? How outrageous is such an act? What did your character think when they found themselves in that predicament in the first place? Could they be so much at a loss that the only thing left for them is to ... what? Perhaps that is the greatest benefit of such a task: helping the actor measure the depth of need they are fighting for. Forget my concerns, maybe the *character* is not concerned with graceful movement at all because they are so desperate to get what they want by the end of the speech? Suppose they genuinely want it that badly? Use your imagination. Just *suppose* ...

Exercise #8: One-Word Beat Change

This is an exercise I love. Normally I use it with two actors working on a scene in acting class but it can also be applied to monologues. To do it with a monologue the actor continues to play the scene, using the full, script-based *subtext* of their speech. Except for this: when speaking they are allowed only *one word at a time* to express their thought and intention. Everything else is the same; they are still caught in an outrageous situation and have to fight for what they want, except they can respond with only one word to their imaginary scene partner.

The same monologue is distilled into a series of single-word responses. Let us consider again the speech of Starbuck from *The Rainmaker*. Using it this way might lead the actor to the following series of utterances:

The actor says:	The subtext means:
Listen!	Stop saying this!
Insult!	You disrespect me!
Rain!	I CAN make it rain!
God!	He BLESSED me!
Normal!	He said I'll never get married or have a family!
Alone!	I won't have a penny to my name!

The single words represent what you *really* want from your scene partner and what you are willing to do, what you *have* to do, to make them give it to you. This exercise is a good way to find out how clear the actor is on their objective. I have seen actors who had already memorized their lines in a scene suddenly get tongue-tied and confused at the prospect of coming up with only *one word* to express those lines to their partner! Why? Because they were not completely clear on what they wanted from the other actor. Lack of clarity made them fall back on the scene itself and try to play the *actual* scene lines, as if trying to visualize the script in their mind's eye. This improvisation is most valuable because it is about listening and expressing need. It can anchor the actor in the here and now: important, no matter how long your monologue is.

Exercise #9: Become the Monologue

Most of the time I use this fun exercise with Shakespeare and other classical pieces that are heavy with descriptive imagery and archaic slang, but it works well for contemporary monologues as well. The idea is for the actor to act out *every image* in the speech as if it were a palpable character, to play them out so fully during the monologue they *become* that image. An example:

In Biff's final monologue to Willy in *Death of a Salesman* he speaks of running down "eleven flights," holding a "pen," seeing "the sky," being a "bum," and refers to his father as a "dime a dozen," who ends up in the "ashcan." With each image in this exercise the actor:

- becomes each *step of the staircase*, maybe stamping up and down eleven times;
- contorts their body into the shape of a *fountain pen*, perhaps squirting across a piece of paper;
- becomes *clouds* in the sky, wafting past above the heavens;
- becomes a *bum*, bent-over, hand-out-begging for pennies, mumbling as if drunk;
- becomes a *silver dime*, a single solitary coin among dozens;
- becomes an *ashcan*, trash barrel, and garbage that is thrown away.

There is no one way to become each of these images, nor is there a wrong way. The actor can discover many fun and imaginative possibilities as long as they do not allow their head to get in their way. What this exercise can do is enliven every moment of the speech and drive the characters' desire to communicate, their *need* to tell their story, through physically demonstrating the images and objects of the speech. How many of these strange, weird actions might the actor finally keep in auditioning with their monologue? I don't know. The fun comes from the genuine child's play when both body and imagination are unleashed to fight for an objective in an outrageous situation. In fact, that is the key: *child's play.*

Exercise #10: Beginning, Middle, End

As you complete work on your monologue, both to 'raise the stakes' and to make it more outrageous, this can be a good final step to help you drive the speech and keep up momentum through the end. You have already built a Beginning, Middle and End into your monologue with the Given Circumstances and the Three Tips from the Script. This last improvisation is meant to make you more active on your feet. It works like this:

1. Reduce the *first third* of your monologue into a *single line*. You do this by simply dividing up the lines into three parts, in whichever way that seems to make sense from your understanding of the speech already, no need to worry if one part winds up with more words than another. As long as you are clear on the objective that best represents each of the three parts you wind up with. This is not unlike the one-word exercise except you are speaking a single declarative sentence that represents the *meaning* of each part of your speech.

   Using the Cherie speech from *Bus Stop* it might work this way:

   > First Part of speech translates to – "I WAS HOT FOR BO AT FIRST!"

2. Next, take the *middle third* of your monologue, where you are stating your case, and do the same thing:

   > Second Part of speech translates to – "BUT HE STOPPED ME FROM RUNNING AWAY!"

3. Finally, reduce the *final third* of your speech, in which you resolve the issues, this way:

   > Third Part of speech translates to – "SO I'M GOING TO MONTANA!"

4. Now take all three of these lines and put them together as if *they* were the monologue and perform them. The "new" monologue is:

   > *"I was hot for him at first. But he stopped me from running away. So I'm going to Montana!"*

   Do this over and over again, building force as you shout ever louder and louder as if you were playing the scene with another character. Allow it to reach a fever pitch crescendo.

5. *Then*, launch into the *real* monologue, acting it as you have rehearsed it before, with all of your understanding of beats, outrageous acts, objectives.

What you are looking for is how this exercise *invigorates the speech and compels you to keep up the pace and communication through the very end of the last line.* Just remember that it is not about volume, it is about the need that propels you. It is always a good idea to double-check the precision of your choices. This improv will help you to do that as well, and may get you even more excited about fighting for what you want in an outrageous situation!

9

MONOLOGUE PITFALLS AND WHAT TO DO ABOUT THEM

I have said this a lot in this book: sometimes in their audition monologues actors play the scene on only one level. This is actually commendable because it can indicate that the actor is committed to really going for it with their performance, doing their best to raise the stakes as high as possible. The auditors will appreciate this from you. But then they will naturally want more – they will want to see you change, they will want to see that you are somehow different at the end than you were at the beginning.

The problem can be with the monologue you picked for the audition. Some speeches, even after all of your analysis and rehearsal, just might be so dependent on the full context of the play from which they came that they can't stand alone. Taken out of context they fail to rise to any other place than what is obvious on the surface, causing your acting to be equally as obvious, with no visible indication that you have been able to bring anything new to the material. I have seen audition monologues that made me think "Why did they pick *this*?"

Here are a few that might fall prey to such pitfalls. They are mostly all good monologues but even the best monologues can seem poor if they are not mined for the changes that will create variety. I have listed possible problems that can crop up in them and a few suggestions you might try to solve them. In the end it may be that you have picked something that simply will not work for you and will not present you to your best advantage, and that the only real solution is to throw it away and find other speeches worth doing, but try these adjustments first.

Some of the suggestions, in an attempt to be outrageous, are not what will always be done with them and in fact they might even be the *wrong* choice to make for the speech. Don't let this throw you; it is intentional. I have said that in rehearsal even what might be found to be the wrong interpretation can lead to something exciting, and with only one minute that excitement is the very thing you want the auditors to see.

Pitfall #1: Only Angry

Rose

Act II, Scene 1

From *Fences*, by August Wilson

Many years ago I had the pleasure of seeing this play during its first run on Broadway with the original cast. Mary Alice delivered this speech to James Earl Jones. It was powerful, electric, explosive, and by the end more than tipping the outrageous scale in its own right. By the end of the scene – and at that moment I could see that it had been building to this point all along – Rose, in a fit of mad love and helplessness, swings her fist at Troy's breast with all of her might, hitting him again and again, pummeling at his barrel chest, even though – perhaps – she had already made the decision to remain with him, and even to raise the child he confessed to her that he was going to have with another woman. There was no question of the impact the scene made upon me – as you can see I remember it vividly to this day; it still gives me goosebumps. If an actress chooses this speech for audition she will not have Troy there to swing her fists at nor will she be able even to speak the speech in its entirety because it is very long as it builds up to this climactic moment. The danger with this speech is that the performer, perhaps rightly, is going to play anger first, and because of the extreme shortness of time – sixty seconds in which to perform it – the audition is likely going to be more about anger than anything else. It can be a great piece for an African American actress with a strong voice and presence as long as the audition is balanced with at least one change, preferably an opposite change, in which the auditors can be allowed to see another side of Rose, a side the auditor had not thought of before. So when viewing this speech in audition I ask myself "*Where is the love?*" In one way or another you will always be asking this question first, especially in a speech that is dramatic. Rose's monologue is long and arduous and builds to a tremendously theatrical moment. With just sixty seconds you don't have that kind of time; you must first release Rose's initial fury and then give them something else, one other side of the talent you've got. To me the natural choice is to present Rose's *love* for Troy. How does the actress do this in such a bitterly resentful monologue? By doing the outrageous. She must display at least a second when she remembers, at the end of the day, that she still loves this unfaithful husband of hers with all of her heart. She loves him!

To do this she might:

Kneel down onto all fours, bowing her head, keening with loving sounds even as her words are of vitriol.

Imagine it. One moment you are shouting at Troy. The next you are on your hand and knees wailing out of love. Is this the right choice? That would be up to the actress in the heat of the moment to decide. I would bet however that it is going to get the auditor to sit up and take notice – of you, and of the variation and range you have just given them. Might it be too far? Maybe. But I am also going to leave that for you to judge after having rehearsed it, having let your acting coach see it. You want to do everything you can that might enrich your imagination as well as your acting.

Pitfall #2: Objective Is Not Big Enough

Ken

Scene 4

From *Red*, by John Logan

I observed this monologue in an audition coaching session and I asked the young actor "What do you want?" Ken has been driven to his wits' end by Mark Rothko, the mercurial painter he is the assistant for. The young actor replied to my question with "Respect." This is one of the pat answers sometimes given when an actor may not be completely clued in on what their character wants specifically but they still somehow sense that at least the character's need is not small. From a theatrical stand-point, respect is a *non-objective* objective; it is a state of being that is conferred, not really a prize won. My answer back to the young man was "What happens if you don't get it? Will you die?" They then have no reply to this because death is not a possibility for them even with the scene being taken out of context. My almost immediate suggestion will be – you have already guessed it – "What happens if you want *love?*" Quite apart from any homoerotic take on the scene the human desire for love is probably the closest thing that comes to a the-atrical magic bullet and universal elixir, the wonder drug for ailing performances. *What if Ken is lashing out at Mark because he is hurt that Mark has not shown him love?* Not necessarily roman-tic love, more like gratitude, appreciation, camaraderie? Then the speech can avoid, yet again, the pitfall of being played with only one action. Suppose Ken, thinking of how much fun and joy and love they have shared working to create art, finds in the monologue just *one* moment – admittedly outrageous and just maybe the wrong choice – when he suddenly starts:

Dancing a jig, kicking up his heels, singing a song?

If you are using this speech I will leave it to you whether this is a choice that is too much. The important thing is what you can discover after having created a change in Ken. If it is not exactly right for where you want to go with the speech at least you have gone there, and other choices, more suitable to your interpretation of the role, will likely be available to you. All because of what is suddenly possible when you are driven to fight for *love* rather than *respect*.

Pitfall #3: You Have to Earn Thoughtfulness

Eurydice

Scene 16

From *Eurydice,* by Sarah Ruhl

Eurydice is a lovely play with several nice monologues, especially for young actors. This particular speech, which comes near the end of the play, has in it the pitfall of falling in love – with *reminiscence,* which can result in it being slow, and at worst even dull. Each time I have seen it done the actress gets dreamily carried away while talking about the man she loves – Orpheus – as she describes the quirky, cute little (as well as large) things he does. Almost without fail this causes her to pause several times, as if suddenly being moved by a thoughtful loving memory. Loving thoughtfulness is a nice thing if you're actually playing the role in performance but for an audition it has got to be more about fighting for something in an outrageous situation. You might be able to display a beat – *only* a beat – of thoughtfulness, but before that you had better dominate the stage driven by a need so great caused by a love so great that, perhaps, the entire speech is *shouted to the rooftops!* Yes, shouted to the rooftops because the love you feel for Orpheus has turned your world upside down! *Then,* in the same way that it is said actors must earn a pause, you might earn a *thoughtful moment* of your character remembering something from their past. One thing the actress can try in rehearsal is:

- SHOUT the monologue without stopping, then –
- pause only ONCE for a beat of thoughtfulness, then –
- BANG! Back to SHOUTING your joy in loving Orpheus!

This speech has made me think of something, and I hope you will indulge me for a quick moment. To me this example of *Eurydice* is an example of the pitfall that can arise when playing the role of Juliet in *Romeo and Juliet.* Actresses cast in this famous role sometimes fall in love with *being in love*, rather than playing Juliet as the thirteen-year-old pistol that she is, full of nerve, piss and vinegar. Juliet, young ladies, is *not* a shrinking vine! If she had been she would never have married Romeo behind her parents' backs, never taken the potion to get out of marrying Paris and never killed herself with Romeo's dagger. Yes, Shakespeare has written the greatest ingénue role of all time with pretty dreamy poetry to spare, but the actress must earn all of those things by portraying a human being caught in an outrageous situation caused by love!

Just my raving from a soapbox. I hope you'll forgive me.

Pitfall #4: The Need for Vulnerability

Starbuck

Act II

From *The Rainmaker*, by N. Richard Nash

(This speech is displayed in "Cutting and Piecing Together Your Monologue.")

This is another speech that can nearly become all about angry yelling. It is so well written, though, with so many opportunities for transitions of character that it is fairly easy to avoid the pitfall. Starbuck is frustrated with Lizzie, the spinster whom he meets on a farm where he has convinced the family that he can cure their drought and bring rain. In the storyline is the very real possibility that Starbuck is nothing more than a snake-oil salesman, no more than bluster and bombast, a question that is not finally answered until the end of the play. Therefore it is not impossible that Starbuck *himself* is not certain that he can bring rain. He realizes that Lizzie seems to have seen through his sham from the beginning and has called him for what he is, a liar and a cheat, challenging him to prove to her family that he has the powers he has claimed. In this scene he lashes out at her not only for her lack of faith in him but in fact for her lack of faith in *anything* – even to the point that she does not accept herself as pretty or attractive to men. The scene ends with him infusing into her so much belief in herself that they share a passionate kiss. It is a wonderful scene from a wonderful play (the subtitle of the play is *A Romantic Comedy in Three Acts*). Starbuck has never been forced to actually confront himself and it is Lizzie who forces him to do it. He thrives on swagger. If you choose to do this monologue you won't be able of course to grab Lizzie and kiss her because she won't be there; to play against so much of Starbuck's bluster you might expose his vulnerable side by playing actions such as to *beg*, to beseech, to *implore*, as a means to portray *self-doubt*. This action can be physicalized by:

- dropping down to your knees;
- throwing yourself prostrate onto the floor;
- curling up at her feet.

This allows Starbuck to plead – an excellent active verb – *plead* to Lizzie to help him avoid being a failure! Play the action of begging to win the objective of getting Lizzie to *believe* in you. Then you will have earned some occasional bluster.

Pitfall #5: Not All Bombast

Black Stache

Scene 7

From *Peter and the Starcatcher*, by Rick Elice

This is a fun speech not unlike Starbuck's, in that the actor might get swept away with being loud, bombastic and theatrical. The difference is that on the face of it the character does not have the love interest and possibility for vulnerability Starbuck has. Black Stache does work well taken out of context, and it allows the actor to play to the 'audience' because he is so taken with himself you can more than imagine that he will get lost in his own big-headedness even while he is talking to Smee. A clear wink in the direction of Captain Hook in *Peter Pan*, Black Stache is luxuriating out loud about his dream that a hero will appear to help him become the great villain he aspires to be. What can give this monologue variety amid the loud theatricality – which you must not lose – is, of course, love. *Love* for the imagined 'hero' that will come into his life and make him complete as a great villain. Suppose the speech is performed with a great *lament* at the absence of such a hero and then *celebrating* the idea of that hero's arrival and then the bitter *attack* at the final discovery that the hero has not yet appeared? These three active verbs, lament, celebrate, attack, will lead Black Stache through a journey that will make him different at the end of the monologue than he was at the beginning of it.

Pitfall #6: When a Monologue Isn't Really a Monologue

From *The Miracle Worker*, by William Gibson

This example is different from the others in that the only real solution is to avoid it completely and pick another monologue. I therefore confess that it's a 'ringer' monologue thrown in just because I want to discuss it with you so that you can avoid this mistake. Once during an audition workshop I conducted at SETC I watched a young actress present this proposed audition monologue taken from William Gibson's *The Miracle Worker*. When she first announced it I was confused, assuming that she had chosen a speech of Annie Sullivan, the title character. Turns out she had chosen the role of Helen Keller's *mother*, who has no substantive monologue in the play! Her 'monologue' had been pieced together from a scene early in the play. Kate Keller approaches her baby daughter's crib, saying 'hello,' when she discovers the child is unresponsive. She calls the baby by name constantly, clapping her hands, finally distraught as she realizes that her infant child is deaf and blind. As I have said I was confused, because when she was done I tried to begin as always with "Who are you talking to?," followed by "What do you want from them?" Neither of these questions would serve her need for coaching; she had chosen a speech so drastically out of context – and so terribly *inactive*, for all of her shouting at the invisible crib – that it was impervious to instruction. The speech was totally a reaction to a stimulus impossible for the auditor to *see*. She had made fatal mistakes on every level; she had chosen a scene in which an imaginary crib is directly *stage left* of her, which she must look into to create an invisible baby, then create the invisible stimulus of the invisible baby being unresponsive, prompting her reaction of horror, most of this causing her body positioning to present *profile* to us for the entire time. End of speech! I suggested to her that she choose another monologue, something that would present her to better advantage by showing her *doing* something to *get* something. All monologues selected from plays for audition are taken out of context, away from their natural heat of actual performance onstage. That's why the actor must fabricate a 'back story' solely for the outrageous situation of the audition. This 'speech' was doomed from the beginning because it was haphazardly pieced together and therefore was not driven by the simplest need to play an objective. Yet this story is still instructive; not only is this a reminder that acting is about doing and not feeling, it also hammers home the fact that if you want to piece together a monologue you must pick a scene in which the character is driven, at least at some point, to speak at *length*.

Pitfall #7: Quiet Is Outrageous, Too

Hannah Jelks

Act III

From *The Night of the Iguana,* by Tennessee Williams

I have mentioned this character before, so here it is. This is a long scene with the possibility to piece together at least two speeches, and all of them have in them the ironic actor's pitfall of *intimacy.* You know actors love to be intimate onstage.

To play realism. What they often forget however is that 'real' onstage is not the same as 'real' in 'real life.' (Or the 'real' of film, which is probably what is on their minds in the first place.) Hannah is sharing a very complicated quasi-sexual experience with Shannon on the porch of a small tourist hotel in Mexico. The imagery is vintage Williams; it is rich, tortuous and vivid – the kind of confession that might be shared by enormously sensitive people in the middle of the night far from home (which is what is actually happening in the scene). As audition material it can appear to fall short in the 'fighting-for' department. Hannah tells the tale of a distant middle-aged man who asked to clutch a piece of her clothing in his hands. Fetishism is of course hinted at here, and though Shannon attempts to prod her into a 'Yuck!' moment Hannah insists, by scene's end, that it was in its unseemly way an expression of love. Those of us who are of a certain age can remember Deborah Kerr's heart-breaking reading of this scene in the 1964 film version, where she had several minutes to deliver it. If you feel that a speech you piece together from this scene can work for you as a chance to display how 'sensitive' and 'honest' your work can be perhaps it will be best if you plan to use it as a second monologue pulled out of your bag at a callback. But you will still have to escape the greatest pitfall of all with this material: the overwhelming temptation to play *mood.* In Part I, "Picking Your Monologue," I suggested being wary of choosing a monologue that is spoken about the past. That is the biggest problem with speeches that happen out of a character remembering something; it can get slow because they seem to be seeing something from far in their past that moved them *then* but not *now.* The result is the performer is taken just as far from *us watching,* as well. Two more challenges:

1. You don't have the full context of the entire play to build gradually to this moment.
2. For a sixty-second audition it might not grab them; you won't have the time.

Please prove me wrong if you still find value in the speech. One thing you might try is this: go all out to present Hannah as a perfectly *ravenous, sex-starved matron*, huffing and puffing, hyperventilating, grabbing onto her own clothing during the memory as if she might very well rip it off of her body, writhing as if to keep talking would tip her onto the brink of an orgasm right then and there! Outrageous? I would hope so. Right for the speech/scene? That is best decided by you. Who knows? Hannah Jelks has a right to want to fantasize about love just like the next gal ...

The monologues listed here are just examples but you might find the same pitfalls in other speeches. The bottom line is that you want to find in them what is *active* and do that, no matter what speech you pick or action you choose.

Summary of "Working on Your Monologue"

1. Read the play your monologue is selected from.
2. Study the Given Circumstances of the play.
3. Study the "Three Tips from the Script."
4. Ask the Stanislavski Questions about your monologue.
5. The final edited or pieced-together monologue must have a clear beginning, middle and end.
6. When blocking your monologue establish a clear playing area center stage.
7. When rehearsing your monologue don't use a chair.
8. Don't choose a speech that requires mime.
9. Even if outrageous exercises are not suitable for your monologue the act of doing them can lead to more believable choices that are just as outrageous.
10. Create variety in your monologue by playing a range of tactics to win your objective. The desire is to present your character going through something that transforms them into a different person at the end of the speech than they were at the beginning.

Part III

PERFORMING YOUR MONOLOGUE

I warrant thee, if I do not act it, hiss me.

The Merry Wives of Windsor

10

AND DON'T FORGET ...

If You Decide to Use a Chair

If you feel that some great dramatic choice is not going to be possible without using a chair bear this in mind: the very act of sitting down is a *pulling back* kind of energy, the very thing you should not do during an audition. You will need to find a way to play against this. When sitting in a chair you are basically cutting your body in *half*, most actors tending to lean forward when seated. This cramps your midsection and diaphragm into themselves, doing the same thing to your vocal production. What may help you with this is if you remain erect so that your midsection won't be so constricted, which you can do by scooting forward nearly to the edge of the seat. You can then look up and we can see you better. This said, I have of course suggested that you not use a chair. But if you must, rehearse it also without. Even though there will more than likely be a chair in the room for your use, you don't want to be thrown by that rare moment when there isn't one.

Placing Your Scene Partner

Don't place the person you are 'talking to' in a chair. Then the speech is about how well you *talk to a chair*. Again, let the speech be about you and how you react to what your imaginary scene partner is *saying*. Place them in the position of standing in front of you even if they *would* be sitting in a chair.

Where Has Your Character Just Been?

The beginning of your monologue may be about "where have you come from?" but the more active choice is if it is about "what has just *propelled* you into this room?" Think of the image of being shot out of a cannon. What has *driven* you to the point that you absolutely must say what you are saying, going through what you are now experiencing, and right before our very eyes?

Where Are You Going?

Of course you will have to end the monologue, and it might include an actual exit (false of course because you will then break character to say "thank you" once completing your audition). There may be a literal context to where you going once you exit already indicated in the script, such as if your character's speech ends with "goodbye!" but you want to motivate your own destination based on the most dramatic needs you can think of. "I must do this now!" What has just happened that forces you to leave the room? What has the person you have been talking to for the past sixty seconds *just said* that drives you into the need to get out of the room? What do you need to *do* or need to *get* that *cannot wait*, that you must accomplish *right now?*

Speaking a Soliloquy

You are never talking *to* yourself. Your character is driven to speak aloud because something they desire *outside* of them is constantly escaping them. To think of the soliloquy as speaking to yourself is to smother the ability to share the monologue; if you are speaking to yourself you are not speaking to *us* out there in the audience. The performance becomes strangely private and introverted, keeping you locked *within* instead of shouting to get *out*. Acting-for-the-Camera classes can unintentionally cause young actors to make this mistake, expecting that the slightest facial nuance the camera lens can pick up will also be seen by a theatrical audience a hundred feet away. This is also why for stage auditions the actor is best to avoid picking a speech from a screenplay; the written dynamics are not the same. When your character is alone you should be at your most presentational, your most *theatrical*. After all, you are in *private*, and able to say out loud what you wanted to say if only you had the chance! If you are by yourself complaining about something that really ticks you off, don't you feel free to let it rip and say what's really on your mind?

Up Good, Down Bad

One of the ways actors trip themselves up, causing them to fail at an audition, is by habitually looking *down*. Because I have seen this so often and try to coach my students against it I have come to call it "Up Good, Down Bad." When an actor is constantly looking downward during their monologue this tells me that somehow they are uncomfortable with either their surroundings or themselves, and they are not clear on exactly what they are doing; this causes them to periodically glance downward, a subconscious expression of uncertainty.

Now I don't mean to say that the actor can never look down during a monologue – perhaps your character has just lost a contact lens and is desperate to find it, or, like the mourners during the final scene in *Our Town*, you are moved to look directly down at the casket of young Emily Gibbs as it is being lowered into the ground. Every single thing you do will catch the eye of the audience; that is why actors in the background during crowd scenes must always be alert and listening; if they should pick their nose for some reason at least somebody in the audience is going to see them and be distracted from the actors speaking. The same thing happens when a character, for seemingly no discernible reason, looks down. In looking down your need to do so has to be so great that it is obvious to your audience; you must be able to insure that their gaze remains on you and your face. The remedy for this habit – you can tell it's coming – is for you to make it absolutely clear what you *want* in the scene and what you *do* to get it. Doing is the anchor an actor can cling to during an audition; it is the solace you can find when trapped in that strange room, nervous out of fear of rejection. Go back and do your homework, asking and re-asking all of Stanislavski's questions. This will also help you to save that special point in the speech when the character honestly *must* look down. Until that moment comes, it never hurts if you 'Cheat Up.' In so doing, along with your facial expressions the auditors will be able to see your character's needs, wants and desires, as well. Audiences find it difficult to understand your words if they cannot see your face.

Up and Down is also about attitude. You have so much further to go if you go *up*; if a character in a speech is in a quandary, look *up* for the direction where they might find an answer, and not necessarily in a religious context (the context of heaven and hell might come to mind for some but you don't have to go there). The very focus *up* is deemed positive, giving, revealing – and it frees the vocal chords, too. *Down* on the other hand is considered faltering, shying away, trying to hide or worst of all perhaps not wanting to do anything at all. If you make a mistake, make it in terms of giving (UP), not taking away (DOWN).

Unintentional Hiding

What actors also do without being aware of it is occasionally making staging or acting choices that cause the auditors to think the actor is hiding from them. An example of this accidental hiding can be technical, such as setting up your imaginary scene partner to your *immediate* left or right, forcing you into too much profile. Another example is acting values that don't seem to be large enough to fill the stage or satisfy the human need required of their character, either in non-specific gestures or timid vocal production or failing to raise the stakes high enough. Theatre requires *size* in need and relationships, and anything so subtle that it won't get past the foot of the stage is hiding. This is also true of acting choices that are *safe* instead of challenging. Plays are not safe! Plays are not about hiding! They are about profound exposure. They are about what happens when what was once hidden *comes to light!*

Rushing

During your audition avoid rushing. Otherwise the only assumption the auditor can make is that you don't really want to be there and you cannot wait to get the whole thing over with. Are you sensing a theme here about wanting to be there? Rushing can become an unfortunate bi-product of the sixty-second cattle call audition; actors feel they have to 'go fast' because they have a limited time to get through their speech. Even if in rehearsal a director gives you a note to 'pick up the pace' – that is, to *go* faster – they are not actually asking for mere speed alone. What they are asking for – and what you want to be the motivating force in your audition monologue – is a visceral *need* that drives you forward because you are so desperate you *cannot wait* to get what you want. This will keep the scene moving and cause you to *appear* to be going 'faster.' Best of all it will also lead you to greater clarity in the playing of your objective.

Don't *Try* to Be Funny

I spoke of this earlier. You shouldn't actually *try* to be funny in a comedic speech. You should not do this even if you are a naturally funny person. Your portrayal must be about a human being caught up in an outrageous situation caused by love, which of course is neither comedic nor tragic, it is *theatrical*. A comic character does not laugh at their predicament; they are driven to distraction by it. Suppose you are the long-suffering young husband in *Barefoot in the Park*? Rest assured, Neil Simon has placed the laughs exactly where they need to be; you do not need to coax them out of the material in order for the audience to get 'Comedy.' In addition, though the comic monologue is constructed to be funny, consider the rich possibility of a speech in which at least a *little* pathos might be injected. Once again: *antithesis*. An example of this is an early monologue spoken by Eugene Jerome in Neil Simon's *Brighton Beach Memoirs*. It is a very funny speech – as most of Simon's monologues are – but it has potential serious tones when he speaks about his Uncle Dave dying of cancer and his grandfather dying of diphtheria (even the word *diphtheria* is funny, isn't it?). Simon brilliantly switches this sadness to hilarity when Eugene goes on to mention his Aunt Blanche's asthma and finally ends with the capping line describing his father's 'high blood pressure!' Most of the job of balancing opposites has already been done by Simon but the actor doing the monologue can experiment with taking at least a moment – *only* a moment, mind you: actually a *beat* – to *mourn* these deaths of his forebears before turning on a dime to properly lighten up the speech at the end. But don't get me wrong here. I am not asking you to make your comedic speech dramatic; it was written to be funny and the audience must be allowed to take it is funny. I am only suggesting a *small* amount of nuance – which can be discovered and tweaked in rehearsal – that might help you find more depth and texture in your performance. If you think I am asking you to aim high with a monologue that is only one minute long, I say: guilty as charged! Give it a try and see what happens. You can always throw out anything that is not working. Though the overall sense of your monologue must be clear you are honestly shown to best advantage if you can display at least some complexity as well, which will do what you really want your performance to do: convince the auditors of the range in your character.

One more thought about the playing of comedy. The character takes the circumstance they find themselves in *completely seriously*. That's where we get the old cliché "Play a comedy like a tragedy and a tragedy like a comedy." It is only the stand-up comic who laughs at their own jokes. When thinking about this I would like for you to remember a famous scene performed by Lucille Ball on one of the episodes of the *I Love Lucy* show. If you are too young to remember the episode I am referring to you can Google "Lucy's Famous Chocolate Scene" on YouTube, for it is a veritable master class on comic acting. The scene is this: Lucy is working on an assembly line at a chocolate factory and it is her task to place the tiny chocolates into their wrapping paper as the pieces pass by her on the conveyor belt. You can already guess where this is going: soon a mechanism in the conveyor belt screws up and the chocolates start rushing past her at a mile a minute, so fast that she cannot possibly pick up each one and put it in its wrapping. Frazzled and panicked, not knowing what to do – and plunged into an outrageous situation! – the only thing Lucy can think of at first is attempting to *eat each one* as they rush by her on the belt and then finally the amazingly funny choice of *cramming as many of the chocolates as possible down her shirt* to get rid of them. The scene is crazy, unbelievable and it works to comic perfection because Lucy is simply doing the best she can in an outrageous situation that for her was *serious business.* That, my dear ones, is how you play comedy.

Crying and Yelling Is Not Dramatic

Sometimes an actor gets the mistaken notion that all they have to do to appear "Dramatic" is to start crying or yelling. This might spark interest from the audience at first but they then lose interest when the character fails to make any other discoveries, a sign that they have not really been affected in some way by their experience. The speech then becomes boring because it has been performed on only one monotonous tone, which is not going to serve the performer's desire to convince the auditors they are a good actor. True, your dramatic speech is serious and may once or twice even require that you explode in a rage or collapse in tears but you can't get away with doing the same thing the entire time. Drama is much more complex than that; it is the conflicted result brought about when a human being is caught in an outrageous situation. We are frail and unpredictable and that makes it possible for us to laugh one moment and cry the next. Our lives are ruled by contradiction and opposites. When picking an audition speech these opposites are what you are searching for and they apply whether the speech is funny or serious: those 'I can't believe I did that!' moments when we shock or delight *ourselves.* If such change does not seem possible in the speech you have chosen, get another speech.

And regarding the Dramatic, it is important that you play against the seriousness that must inevitably come. I do not mean that you should look on every scene in *The Diary of Anne Frank* as a laugh riot (although a *bit* of properly injected humor, truthfully, is not going to hurt). I mean that your character should *not know* that something bad or tragic is going to happen. If they do, they should fight as hard as they can to prevent it from happening. This will help your character to remain as *positive* as possible about their circumstance for as long as possible, which will create greater impact on them when tragedy finally hits. In the make-believe that is good acting it will also create what actor/playwright William Gillette called "The Illusion of the First Time." There may be instances of foreboding and foreshadowing in the script before tragedy strikes but we do not want bad things to happen and we try our best to *trick* ourselves into believing that they won't happen. How certain was Oedipus of his fate before he found out that he was the one who had in fact killed his father Laos?

Go Somewhere and Take Us with You

With your audition take us – and *yourself* – on a journey. At least *somewhere*. Even though it may be as short as sixty seconds the audience wants to feel as though they have gone on some expedition with you, an expedition through your life struggle: making acting decisions that take the character through some outrageous trial that will change them by monologue's end. How do you do this? How do you take us on a 'journey?' By fighting to find as many solutions as you can for the outrageous obstacles that stand in your way. The movement of the speech, the journey, happens because you are changing *tactics*, or *active verbs*, beginning first with those that make the most sense and then – because you are desperate – reaching for the tactic/verb that is as outrageous as the situation your character is in. This change, this constant trial and error – I haven't forgotten that you only have sixty seconds – is what makes them a new person by the time they have come out of it. And by 'coming out of it' I don't mean that they have won. I only mean that it is over for *now*.

If in Doubt about Your Choices

As you work on a monologue, trying to make it outrageous and to sell you to best advantage, these suggestions may be of help.

- If a speech is fundamentally positive find possible moments of the *NEGATIVE*.
- If a speech is fundamentally negative find possible moments of the *POSITIVE*.
- Always look for an expression of *LOVE* in a monologue.
- Always look for the *BAD POINTS* in the Hero.
- Always look for the *GOOD POINTS* in the Bad Guy.

When to Stop Your Monologue

Many times I have seen auditions in which I wished the actor had stopped speaking sooner or sung a few bars less of their song. It seemed that logical stops were indicated in the material I was hearing and in the work that I was seeing. As soon as this went on I began to listen for the *next* place that they might stop, and then the *next* and ... I don't want to throw a wrench into the works but I would like to offer another consideration about how you might finish your audition monologue. It can be that you will serve yourself if you stop your speech or song a touch sooner than you think might be necessary: say at fifty to fifty-five seconds instead of sixty, for instance. Don't get me wrong here; I am not suddenly changing the rules, changing a sixty-second audition time into fifty. Those sixty seconds will be more than amply filled by your performance. Stopping sooner than your allotted time just might cause the auditors *to want more* by the time you are finished. This doesn't mean that you aren't giving yourself body and soul to that audition, it only means that you are not pulling every arrow out of your quiver, and that you have much more in store for them *if they call you back.* There is a danger of looking desperate if you seem to be giving every last ounce of what you've got. You wouldn't do that even in performance of a play; you would pace yourself during the evening so that you have something left for the end. If you lop off a millisecond or two even your own breathing and humanity will more than fill the interim. And the auditors, if they liked you, will want to see what else you can do.

Also beware of 'saving the big moment' for some presumed big pay-off, which I have talked about. Times have changed. For regional theatre audition appointments five minutes is a common allotment of time to do two monologues. Now two-and-a-half minutes for a single speech seems like forever. Today an audition monologue that is projected to be 'long' is best edited to a run time of ninety seconds at the most. This allows ample opportunity for an internal voyage of change without feeling rushed. For the sixty-second speech it is possible that fifty-five seconds – with the understanding that non-verbal reaction and 'feeling it' are left to finish out the remaining five seconds – just might be *plenty.*

11

AUDITION!

You have properly rehearsed your monologue. Now it is time to audition.

For the unified audition such as you will find at the SETC Annual Convention you will be led into a ballroom with other auditionees to wait your turn as a group, then you will be taken from that room into the ballroom where the actual auditions for the theatre companies are held. You will be sitting with some forty other actors as you wait your turn to step up onto the stage to audition. Some actors find great trepidation at this wait, being forced to watch all of their rivals ahead of them perform. Because certain speeches can get popular and in fashion (as well as some songs) it is not impossible that you may hear a few people doing the same monologue; stories have been told about actors suddenly hearing an actor in front of them performing the very same monologue *they* had prepared. I have witnessed this myself. Still, it is possible for your tensions to ease once things get started because you will realize right away just how wide the variety is of actors and actor/singers waiting to be seen; a competitive side of you may kick in and you might be moved to think "Well, all right. Let's see what you got. I bet mine is better than yours!" Once calm, you might even be able – and wise – to listen for a particular speech that you like and want to steal to use later. In any event take this time before the audition, while you are nervously waiting, to study and learn. Outside of your own performance there is no greater way to find out what the acting audition experience is really about. Before that hectic day, as part of your rehearsal process and even as a last-minute mental check as you wait in the ballroom, keep reminding yourself of a few things.

What the Sixty-Second Monologue Must *Do*

With your monologue you are trying to prove:

- you can act;
- you can speak;
- you can sing pretty, OR at least SELL (ACT) a song;
- you can move reasonably well (*not* dancing).

How Much Can They Really See in Sixty Seconds?

Everything. Do not kid yourself. This is one of the many cruel audition truths. From the moment you walk onto the stage auditors can actually decide whether or not they like you. At least instinctually. Then it is the audition itself that 'seals the deal.' Excluding assessment of your monologue they can tell this through several unfair tip-offs, such as:

- if you don't step onto the stage with energy and authority;
- if your posture is poor and you slump rather than stand up straight;
- if you do not smile;
- if you often look down for no visible reason;
- if you fail to speak up with an assertive voice and are barely audible, losing energy at the end of a sentence (amazing as it may seem actors sometimes speak so softly the auditors cannot even hear their *name*, let alone their monologue!);
- if you:
  - are wearing loud-colored, unflattering clothing;
  - are wearing too-short skirts or too-low necklines;
  - have wrinkled, dirty-looking clothing;

- have your hair in your eyes;
- have bizarre makeup;
- present yourself in any way that distracts from your audition;

- if you seem to rush the end of the monologue and the "thank you" as you depart. This gives the impression that you want to get offstage in a hurry.

Of course all of this is outrageous. Even more so because it is true – and necessary. Your mere presence in the room is sending them all of these messages. Watch a few hours of unified auditions for yourself sometime and you will discover this. It is wise to rehearse your entrance and introduction as much as you rehearse your speech, and to do all you can to insure that your appearance is presented with as much professionalism and good taste as possible.

Dress and Hygiene

For Men

- Hair well-groomed and combed away from your face, especially if your hair is long enough to require being tied back into a pony tail.
- Clean-shaven if no beard.
- Neatly trimmed if you have a beard.
- No shirttail out.
- No low-ride 'gangsta' jeans; as a matter of fact, no low-ride *anything*.
- No jeans with holes in them.
- No dirty sneakers.
- No sandals or flip-flops: hard-heeled street shoes. *Shined.*
- Nothing wrinkled.
- Slacks and pressed shirt; jacket and tie optional but they never hurt.
- Remember you are at a job interview.

For Women

- Street makeup that makes you look good is sufficient. Not too heavy.
- Hair pinned or tied back away from your face.
- No wild hair color.
- No miniskirts. Knee-length or below.
- No plunging neckline.
- No wild, obtrusive jewelry.
- No slacks. You can always wear them later at a callback if for a particular role, such as Rosalind in *As You Like It* or Sylvia the dog from the play *Sylvia*. However, if you truly believe that you look best in slacks and have to have them for the initial audition make sure they are not too tight, are long enough and are not some wild color.
- No sandals or flip-flops.
- No boots.
- No clogs or platform shoes.
- No stilettos.
- Preferably a heel no higher than a character shoe.
- No wild colors; they can be obtrusive.
- No black dress; some venues have a black curtain on the stage behind you and this will cause you to disappear.
- Wear stockings.
- You are on a job interview; a suit will not hurt.

Final Clothing Thoughts

Taste and style will vary. It is also true that something that makes you look bad knows no season; sad to say some folks put on the most horrific clothes, tie up their hair in the most ridiculous ways, and still think they look good. If you are not certain what to wear ask a friend or better yet ask your teacher/acting coach. Bring in a few choices for them to see. The bottom line is that in addition to looking good and presentable you are trying to accomplish two things: first to look *professional*, like you are taking both the auditors and yourself as serious, and second to avoid anything with dress that will by its visual take *away* from their ability to be caught up in the story the monologue represents. In short, you want their concentration on *you*.

Lastly I will take the risk, and am willing to take the politically incorrect heat, by saying this: the Type performers are also trying to sell at an audition is their *gender*, which, like it or not, translates to *sexuality and sex appeal*. Plays rely upon and demand that a man look like a man and a woman look like a woman. I am talking about leading man/male ingénue roles and leading lady/female ingénue roles, written for romantic interest. With male or female character-actor roles – 'best buddy'/'side kick' parts – sex appeal usually will not be as crucial, though clear lines of gender are still important. You are selling this part of yourself as well.

Tattoos

This thought is for both men and women. Your body is your own, to do with as you please. That said, please consider this: in seeking to be an actor, especially for the stage, your desire is to prove to an audience that you can become *anyone, anywhere, anytime*. While some tattoos might be the kind that would only be seen if you were naked, a visible tattoo screams out loud that you are unquestionably of and from the *present* day. I say this not to trample on your right to individuality. Put yourself in the place of any potential employer who does not know you in the corporate workplace – and yes, take note of the fact that I choose to use the word *corporate*. Because theatre is an artistic enterprise it can accept people from any walk of life without concern for what they look like. This is true. But the rules are different for employees who will be often in the public eye – such as *actors*; as with any business that wants to survive in the marketplace these employees have to play by certain rules. Remember what I said earlier about not using profanity in an audition, even though many of the very people judging you might use it all of the time in their workaday lives? The same is true of actors presenting themselves in the professional world. It is perfectly reasonable to suspect that once in rehearsal you can dress in whatever way you feel comfortable and appear as grungy and unkempt as you wish. But to get to that point you first have to jump through the hoops of professional conduct required of an organization in the public sector at large. Actors must convince potential employers that they are capable of depicting *another culture entirely*, and at the job interview (the audition) these employers cannot imagine you this way if your physical appearance gets in the way of their admittedly rushed analysis. Once a director gets to know you they can allow a lot more individuality. They can allow the nose ring or tongue stud because they know you will take them out for performance; they can get past wild hair color because they know you can be wigged or you are willing to rinse it to a more conservative color for the show. I once worked with a fine actress who worked constantly in regional theatre; after being in the business for a few years she chose out of convenience to wear her hair cut short like a boy, sometimes changing its color from jet black to snow white. She worked all the time. Why? Because through her *work* she proved that she was talented, professional, and she didn't cause any problems for the theatre company she worked for. Directors who originally gave her a chance realized that she could be wigged for a play if necessary. This was years into her career, after she had eschewed the traditional long hair she had begun her career with. So it's possible through proving yourself to earn a little leeway. It's just that when first starting out you must be more conservative. I will say this once more: *your body is yours to do with what you will.* But to begin your acting career – even in the theatre, which embraces all kinds of people – an actor will serve themselves best if they look professional and, dare I say, 'neutral': a blank canvas upon which the full range of dramatic characterizations can be painted with their talent. You will earn more freedom with your appearance – within reason, of course – after directors get to know how good and reliable you are. In the meantime, though, if you cannot rely upon a

theatre company to produce a wild, modern-dress interpretation of a play stop and ask yourself: Men, where is Hamlet's
body tattoo? Ladies, where is Ophelia's nose ring?

The Audition Step by Step

Step One: Entrance

Rehearse your entrance as much as your speech. As you enter
smile (genuinely!) and take in the room, surveying the stage
floor to mentally prepare the boundaries for your performance. You are looking ahead of you to center stage, toward what
will become the depth and width of your personal 'stage.' You
might even be looking for the distant EXIT sign at either the
direct rear of the auditorium or ballroom, or you are looking
to your left or right if your performance requires these directions for focus.

Step Two: Find Your Light

This is one of the oldest of the stage actor's tools of training: making sure that you are in proper light to be seen. Every
actor worth their salt who wants to go onto the stage ought to
be able to do this. It is actually simple; as you step onstage look
directly up toward the lights hanging above you and stare into
what appears to be the brightest, most intense center beam of
light streaming from either the Fresnel or Ellipsoidal lamp,
almost bright enough to make you see spots. Shift yourself
from side to side, taking note of when the light appears to pass
you, in either direction, and shift back until the light seems to
be at its 'hottest' on your face. Believe it or not you will actually
imagine that you can feel the light 'warm' on your face. Then
you can trust that you are in proper light. You will get better at
this the more often you have the chance to do it. I realize that
your time will be short and precious but take the time to do
this if the stage is an auditorium with the house lights either
low or turned off (most likely to help the actors the lights will

all be turned up full anyway). In a ballroom all of the lights will
be on. As a matter of fact, do this: go into the theatre on your
own campus and have a technician or your teacher turn on the
stage lights for you. Then, give it a try. It will be helpful to have
your acting teacher/coach watch to reassure you that you are
getting it right. Do it a few times: walk out on the stage to center
and looking up to the lights to find your place. Auditors find it
tiresome when the actor is so 'into it' during their audition that
they move so far in one direction that they place themselves in
relative darkness. On the other hand – and you truly will learn
how to do this faster as you get the hang of it – they will understand and appreciate a performer professional enough to know
that they have to be in proper light, and savvy enough to make
sure of it before they begin. It only takes a few seconds.

Step Three: Go to Center

Place yourself center, within the imaginary perimeter you have
established during rehearsal. You will also be looking directly at
the audience; this is all right because you have not commenced
your audition yet and are not making them a part of your performance. Think of this as visually 'shaking hands' with them
with your eyes and warm smile, the very same way you would if
meeting them in an office for a job interview. If you are using a
chair (NOT recommended) you will be moving it quietly into
place, naturally center.

Step Four: Focus Points

This is very important. It is said – and I concur – that you should
avoid playing your monologue directly to the auditors because
you then place them in the unenviable position of *playing your
scene with you.* This is not what they are there for. They want to
be free and unbridled so that they can look at you and observe
whether they think you are any good or not, *and* they want to
be able to glance down at your résumé to make notes – such
as "Call this person back." The kind of room you are in will
affect this so start by setting your focus just above the heads of

the people watching you. It will help keep you pointed toward them without looking directly at them. This is particularly necessary with the soliloquy, in which your character is alone and fighting for something outside of themselves. Set your focus and do not stray from it; you look like an amateur when your field of vision wavers during the audition.

The Actual People in the Audition Room

While you don't want to look directly at the directors and producers observing your audition there is actually another thought to consider. I once served as Adjudicator for Screening Auditions for SETC in South Carolina. Instead of a large auditorium or small studio the auditions were held in a medium-size lecture hall with raked rows of seats in the auditorium and a faintly oval 'stage' at the bottom. Approximately 250 seats: not too large or small. Lights up the entire time. As I was watching, being reminded of so many of the points I am trying to make in this book, I gained more insight on the actor auditioning for a group of strangers. These considerations will work well in particular when the audition venue is not massive and the lights remain on, which tends to make for a more intimate atmosphere between actor and auditor.

- As long as you do not play your scene *directly* to the auditors a pleasant, beginning look in their eyes as one human being to another is not bad and might even help to relax you.
- After you have seen them and they have seen you back you may *then* begin your audition, and it is at this point that you seek to avoid their gaze. Actually it is not unlike the 'slating' of yourself before a film take. For focus on the stage with the lights off you do not have the obvious challenge of looking the auditors directly in the eye, yet there are some speeches that will be so large in tone they will benefit from the performer 'playing the house.' This is the case with monologues like the 'St. Crispin's Day' speech from *Henry V,* for instance, or St. Joan before her inquisitors, or any monologue in which the character is clearly breaking

the fourth wall. Holding to the left-center-right set-up will prevent your focus from wavering side to side. Besides, if the character is speaking directly to the audience to begin with, shouldn't you actually *be* looking at the audience?

Your Imaginary Scene Partner

Who are you talking to? Are they with you in the present setting? Or are they not actually there in the script and you are speaking as if they were? Don't let your monologue become a ghostly alien world in some other universe; establish right from the play and the Given Circumstances exactly where your character is and to whom your character is speaking. Even if the person who is meant to hear what you have to say is not there you will still play it as if they were, with all of the force of your human need. Do we not do this in real life? When you are speaking to a mirror in order to get up the gumption to ask your boss for a raise or ask your girl to marry you do you not still honestly *plead your case?* Your audition monologue is the same kind of plea. Once rooted in your invisible four-to-five-foot circumference stay in that circle and you won't likely wander too far in either direction and out of the light (for obvious reasons you will be establishing this space on the stage in the light they provide). Unless your performance demands great animation you need not move that much during the speech anyway. In addition be aware and alert so that you do not get so 'into it' during your performance that you forget yourself and wander so far downstage that you nearly fall off. I have seen this almost happen before and it is not a cliff-hanger you want to create. Play your scene with the 'person' you are talking to and stay focused there.

Step Five: Announce your Name and Number

At most cattle call auditions you will have a number in addition to your name. In a clear, projected voice announce your name and your number. You might consider this your first real hurdle because it is the first time you will have opened your mouth to speak since being called in from the holding room. If you have to clear your throat in any way please do it as unobtrusively as possible while you sit waiting for your turn, or maybe as you get up to move toward the stage. It is not necessary to announce the monologue or the play from which it came; this will only take away from your precious time. They start timing you the moment you begin to speak.

My view is keep your announcement as short and professional as possible. Emphasize *professional.* This means that you do not want to say anything that will smack of the amateur. Never say "I will be *performing* a scene from ..." or "This is the scene *where* ...." These statements make the auditors think of community theatre where more than likely the viewer has only a limited knowledge of plays and playwrights. Personally I even have a problem with even using the word, '*piece*,' or '*monologue.*' I have two suggestions for your announcement:

For the sixty-second audition it is not necessary (and is a time waster) to mention the character and play, but sometimes you might be auditioning for a full season at a repertory company. Then you probably have an individual appointment and two speeches of greater length then sixty seconds have been asked for. In this case you will say:

Hello. My name is John/Jane Doe. This is (Character Name) from (Title of the Play).

If you have chosen a speech from one of the great roles such as Stanley Kowalski or Lady Macbeth you can simply give the character name. They will know the play. Like this:

Hello. My name is John/Jane Doe. This is (Character Name).

If you are at one of the unified auditions and have a number to mention do it this way:

Hello. My name is John/Jane Doe. Number 000.

Short and sweet. In announcing your monologue you are doing much more than telling the auditors what your number is and what you will be performing. You are telling them that you are a professional who wants to be there, who is happy to be there.

Final Note: make sure that during the entirety of your performance you *breathe*. This might be so obvious that it is overlooked, which is why I mention it here. In the nervous emotional throes of the audition experience, especially when you might be more concerned about getting everything to fit into a sixty-second time limit, it is possible sometimes to forget the one thing that may serve you most of all and if forgotten can derail you: breath control. It is not being too persnickety to even go through your text and write in exactly *where* you can best take a breath and where you need to keep speaking through the line, etc. Rehearse these breaths as much as your monologue itself. Have you ever heard of opera singers fainting dead away because their knees were locked, causing hyperfusion of the brain?

Step Six: Perform

This is the moment you have been waiting for. It is your time to act, to 'show 'em your stuff!' As stated in this book I am not in favor of taking a moment to 'get into it' before you begin. You ought to be 'into it' the moment you enter the room, the moment you arrived that very morning. Do your 'getting into it' outside of the audition room before going in. As a matter of fact, the question of being 'into it' ought to have been established the moment you decided you were going to audition in the first place. Spare your auditor the stagey "I'll turn my back now and then turn around and wow you because I've suddenly *become* somebody else!" When you do the 'turn around' or 'bow your head' thing it sets up the expectation that whatever happens when you finally do turn back *is going to be wonderful* – so it had better be! Avoid this. I realize that you are doing it to 'focus' before you begin and you must do that, but should not that focus have already happened? Doing this can suggest that you were not 'ready' when you came in. Such a block-buster after a turned back and bowed head rarely happens; if you are good enough to produce that kind of a reaction after doing this more power to you, but I have never seen it happen. Warm up properly and completely as you wait *outside* the door so that when your name is called to go in you are, essentially, *already* doing your monologue as you smilingly enter the room! This is what I am talking about when I speak of knowing exactly when your monologue begins. The nervous energy you will understandably be feeling while waiting for your time to audition can be channeled into the beginning of your speech. Then you just might 'wow' them.

Still, I have to admit that the 'bowed-head focus thing' is done and it probably does not bother too many of the auditors who are watching (they aren't old fuddy-duddies like me). It is after all a theatrical convention. Though you will discover that sixty seconds is ample time to perform, remember that one minute is still one minute magnified a hundred times in our sensory observation of you: every breath you take; every gesture, planned and unplanned; every vocal utterance; and every single second of those sixty that we are called upon to watch you is on display.

All of the above said, let me clarify one thing. While you should be ready to launch into your speech at any moment, it is more than acceptable and still important to allow for a hair's breadth of time to 'take in' what has forced your character to speak to begin with. This is quite apart from completely turning your back to 'get into it.' Something has just been said to you or done to you that *demands you respond*. As long as that is the case before you begin your speech, you will still be in the moment, driven by the outrageous situation your character has been plunged into by the playwright. And, most importantly, you are still able to use those precious seconds to prove how good you are when the curtain goes up.

Step Seven: Finish

At the end of your monologue take the barest millisecond of a pause – a *beat* – to make it clear to the auditors you have finished your performance. During this break you are relaxing your body and face back to center – by 'center' I mean a state of emotional well-being, not your physical place on the stage. You are returning to the nice, well-groomed young person who entered the room smiling and confident little more than a minute ago.

Step Eight: Repeat your Name and Number, and Exit

Having clearly finished and relaxed yourself back to center you will again announce your name and number, and you will exit. Rehearse this last bit as well, even the moment when you turn to leave. It is not preposterous to say that even your *back* muscles – yes I know it sounds crazy but I am serious – will be performing as well, even though hidden inside your clothing, reminding everyone how assertive and happy you are to have been there. This is how long you 'stay in character.' Make no mistake: you are communicating to the auditors countless messages about you as a performer even as you exit the space, the stage and the room. It may be that you will be able to relax after you have returned to your seat. However if I were you I wouldn't take any chances there, either ...

When Does the Audition End?

When you exit the audition room. If you get a callback the process will start all over again (after you have caught your breath of excitement over the news that you got a callback, of course).

What Directors Want to See at a Callback

Assuming you might be what they are looking for they will call you back. They are looking for more than talent at this callback. They are trying to get an inkling, face to face, of:

- Your range: that is, how wide is the range of roles you can play?
- Your personality: do you seem like a 'nice person who won't cause me any problems?'
- Your mutual acquaintances who might be contacted to get the real scoop on you.
- Your training: how well have you been trained?
- Your experience: have you done a lot of roles or just a few?
- Your availability: can you start rehearsal at any time?
- Your ability to take direction if they offer you an adjustment to your monologue.

What Is It Like to Audition?

I admit it is probably folly to speak about the actual audition experience itself. Just the same I would like to give it a try. In truth it is going to be like every theatrical performance; you will be nervous before you do it, and in the middle of doing it there will be fleeting moments of awareness and connection to material and impulse, and then immediately afterward you will feel that it seemed unbelievably fast and that it went by far too quickly. If you are lucky there may be a hint of instinct within you that the choices you made were successful; somehow you might just *feel* that it went well. On the other hand if not you will be in the uncomfortable position of trying to mentally re-trace every step of the audition in your mind, going over it again and again in the hope of reassuring yourself that in fact you did do what you had planned and that it did go well. In the end however you know in your heart that the only thing that will really reassure you will be a callback. Otherwise memory of the audition will stay with you, constantly nagging you, until you get word of the play being already cast or another audition has mercifully taken its place to help you forget about it.

As with most actors it will probably be when the audition is truly over – after you say "thank you" – when you suddenly realize all the things you *should* have done with the monologue. This revelation will not comfort you in the near term, of course, but it can help as you prepare for the next audition. In fact this can become the best news of all: when you finally realize, after this trial by fire, that you actually *want* there to be another audition!

Being so glad to get that next audition is the surest way for you to know that you are hooked on a career in theatre.

Summary of "Performing Your Monologue"

1. Fight for something in your monologue.
2. Play the opposites in your monologue.
3. Choose a monologue that presents you at your best, as you uniquely are.
4. Play the love in your monologue.
5. Rehearse your entrance into the audition room and your introduction as well as your exit.
6. The auditors can detect everything about you as you step onstage and even before you speak.
7. Set the position of your imaginary scene partner downstage of you.
8. Set the focus to the rear EXIT sign of the audition room or just above the heads of the auditors so that you are not playing your monologue directly to them.
9. Both men and women, dress professionally and seek advice on choice of clothing.
10. Both men and women, consider avoiding visible tattoos because they limit the kind of roles you can play.
11. The sixty-second monologue is meant to prove your ability to act, speak, sing and move.
12. The auditor uses the callback to find out if you will fit into their theatre company as well as if you can act.

Part IV

"JUST A FEW NOTES FOR YOU"

O Lord, I could have stay'd here all the night
To hear good counsel: O, what learning is!

Romeo and Juliet

I can recall many years ago being taken under the wing of older, more seasoned actors. They were all wonderfully kind and they loved, in their own way, to talk about their craft. What this would lead to – thank goodness – was their putting me wise to the world of acting and show business, often passing along a few pearls of wisdom, 'notes,' to help my fledgling performance. One of the first such notes I can remember is "Act *on* the line." I share this little 'gem' with my students to this very day.

Included here are many other such notes, which apply to theatre in general as well as auditioning and performing in particular. You have probably heard a lot of them before in your travels. That's as it should be. It only proves how perceptive and helpful were the generous people who took the time to share them with me so long ago. It reminds me that, no matter what the human endeavor, the teacher–pupil relationship has been going on for a long time, and it should be cherished. Wonder who it was that first took Aristotle aside?

12

REHEARSAL NOTES

We have talked about how to get you ready to audition using a sixty-second monologue to get an acting job. If you have been cast – and I hope you have been – I would like for you to consider the thoughts in the next two chapters as you rehearse and play a role onstage.

Make the *Visceral* Choice

Even if there is no bloodshed onstage, every choice the actor makes should be, literally, about flesh and blood. The desires of the human heart faced with overcoming an outrageous situation can concoct all kinds of fantasies, and not a few of them that result either in horrific violence or, more importantly, the *dream* of horrific violence. In the mind of a character there ought to be at least the possibility of the scene ending with spilt blood. This is available to the actor in virtually any play, even in the plays of Anton Chekhov, where to some it might seem that nothing happens except people sit around talking about doing something they never get done. His play *Uncle Vanya* climaxes with a hilarious scene of the title character chasing after another character firing at them with a stolen pistol. Vanya misses, causing us in the audience to howl with laughter, but at the same time what motivated his action was, for him, dead serious. In a more dramatic example Chekhov's lesser-known play

Ivanov ends with the title character dashing offstage to shoot himself. That is literally in the stage directions, and then the curtain comes down. This visceral human reaction is the same whether the play is a comedy or a tragedy, and in many plays the bloodshed is not only imagined in the character's mind – we get to see it onstage. We see it to great musical effect in *Sweeny Todd: The Demon Barber of Fleet Street,* in which victims' throats are cut onstage, and in *Little Shop of Horrors* as we witness a man-eating plant gobble up body parts and the rest of the characters whole. And don't forget the classics, such as our first tragedy, *Oedipus the King,* in which the title character appears onstage in the final moments of the play having gouged out his own eyes; and Shakespeare's *Titus Andronicus,* where the audience is 'served up' a villainous queen made to eat her own children baked into a pie (the play also contains the horrific vision of Titus' young daughter emerging onstage after being raped, her tongue cut out)! Outrageous choices are at the actors' disposal when they are willing to ask themselves: if bloodshed really could result at the end of a scene – what would your character *do* to avoid it?

Need the Other Person

This is one of the most important acting notes, which I also refer to as a *positive* choice. A positive choice is not about your character being happy or a good person. It is about making a choice that causes you to *need* the other person in the scene. Plays and drama are about people who MUST communicate; who MUST talk; who MUST fight, love, seek the truth together. When your character says to another "I don't want to talk to you. Leave me alone!" what they probably mean is "We MUST talk and settle this thing right here and now!" The only time you can truly believe that a character doesn't want to talk to another is if the playwright has written it into the script that they *exit the room.* If a character seems to be cold and stand-offish toward another character think of such action as *sending that person a message.*

Look on their coldness as a *tactic* through which they will gain the chance to confront the other person, to set the stage for the argument, lay the groundwork for the coming inevitable fight with their adversary. Do we not do this in real life? For example, if a person is upset with something their spouse has said or done and feels that it has not been resolved, is it not possible that they might give their partner the 'cold shoulder,' sitting at the breakfast table staring at the morning newspaper rather than engaging their spouse? When in doubt always go back to the script; if your character remains in the scene and carries on a conversation with the other character this means the playwright wants the two of you to talk for some important reason, no matter what outward appearance might initially be presented.

You Don't Have to Look at Your Scene Partner All the Time

Allow the needs of a speech to take you away from the other actor's gaze. This is because you are fighting for something that is hard to reach because it is outside of you. We do this all the time when we are moved to reminisce with a friend; in this regard we 'see' that past memory that we are speaking of, whether it is pleasant or unpleasant, and we cannot resist looking back at ourselves, reflecting on how we were then. Your scene partner is human too and will understand because they have also been caught up in such a reverie before. When talking with a friend who suddenly drifts away from us to a moment in their past we are taken to the same moment – in *our* past.

Negative

Avoid making a negative choice. A negative choice is not only one that is angry or contentious; it can also be unintentional, when the actor does something in a scene that prevents them from fully engaging their scene partner or the audience. In the case of the audition such a choice might cause the auditor to get the feeling that you are uncomfortable, that maybe you fear what you are about to do is not really any good. In the audition a negative choice can be manifest in the form of body language, such as:

- appearing uncertain or hesitant as you step into the room;
- habitually looking down;
- losing energy at the end of a line;
- mumbling the consonants;
- gestures that appear to be lock your elbows into your sides;
- gestures that freeze the fingers of your hands into 'paddle' shapes;
- avoiding eye contact with the auditor even upon coming into the room.

These symptoms can be fixed by rehearsing your entrance and the introduction of your monologue with your acting coach. Practicing this bit of stage 'business' will help to anchor you as you come into the room and prevent any negative messages.

A negative choice in a scene is when you fail by your actions to include the other character or do not do what causes you to need them in the scene. Unfortunately this can happen when some actors seem to be selfishly playing only to the audience, as if to win favor for their performance rather than honestly playing with their partner; it can also happen, just as selfishly, if an actor appears to be constantly upstaging the other actor, projecting their responses in such a way that causes the other actor to have to turn their back to the audience to listen or reply (this last one, however, usually does not go on for very long before your scene partner either goes to the director to complain about it or before, just maybe, they punch you in the nose for your discourteous breach of theatre etiquette!). But these examples are more likely to happen among more experienced actors who are in theatre for more egotistical, self-serving reasons. For the most part the negative choice occurs accidentally, like the bulleted examples above. I will replay my broken record: in the rehearsal process the way you fix these problems is by delving back into your script and finding stronger, more specific active verbs so that you are absolutely clear on what you are *doing* in the scene!

Remember that scenes in plays are only incidental if one character exits the room; otherwise you can trust that at least some vital point of the story is going to come from your character engaging the other. Believe it or not it is possible, even in an audition where you are alone, to actually appear to shrink away from your *imaginary* scene partner! If you are not sure if you are doing this the best thing to do is to have your acting teacher or coach observe. They can tell you if these habits creep in and can help to pull you out of them.

'Kind of' Choices Lead to 'Kind of' Acting

Related to the negative choice and occurring just as unconsciously, this happens when the actor fails to be specific in how they *name* their action. Semantics matter. More than in life a character in a play genuinely wants what they want or they don't. This is true even if the character says "I'm so confused!"

There are words beginning actors chronically use when asked to describe their objective, and although they do not realize it the unspecific words can directly affect their execution of the scene. Words and phrases to be banished from the young actor's vocabulary include:

- kind of;
- like;
- sort of;
- just, as in "I'm *just* ...";
- basically;
- you know.

These are called "filler words," when the person speaking inserts words to 'fill' the space until they can think of what they really want to say. Actors who speak this way are stalling until they can think of the right words to name their objective or action.

These words are telltale signs that the actor has to go back to the drawing board. None of these, in practice, is going to make the scene happen because they are too vague. In particular, the word *like* seems to be the special favorite among my young students. I have heard it used multiple times in just *one sentence!* To deliver your strongest performance it is best to decide that a certain thing *is* something rather than being *like* something else. Find out the true meaning and do *that*. Think Metaphor rather than Simile. If you know exactly what you want and what you are doing you are going to be at your most powerful and free of inhibition, and then the scene will be able to take off.

To 'Get Information' Is Not Specific Enough

"How are you today?"
"Fine."
"Good."

You have just gotten information. Big deal.

It matters how you state your objective. Make a choice that will compel outrageous behavior out of you and it will likely compel the same out of the person you are speaking to. This can be hard at first because some choices sound sexier than others; *to get information* is not as likely to provoke action as, say, *to make them grovel at your feet*. Suppose you are playing a cop who has been given the task of interrogating a prisoner. On the face of it you might *appear* to be trying to 'get information'; however, careful study of the play – coupled with the willingness to take acting risks – will lead you in another direction. Suppose the prisoner has shot your partner. On the face of it in the scene it might appear that you are required to ask questions of the prisoner to find out what happened, but in reality you might want to *get revenge*, right? If they give you lip you may want to *put them back in their place*, yes? Even if neither of these things has happened you will need to find out the intrinsic needs of the scene, what is driving your character from within rather than just what seems to be happening on the surface. In other words, *subtext*. If your character asks a few questions and then exits the room you can believe that the action of getting information will suffice. For the scene in which two characters clearly engage one another more is going on between them than that. It is your job to find out that 'more.'

To 'Get Respect' Is Not Strong Enough

Respect is a laudable good thing but in and of itself it is not dramatic or interesting. Will you die if you don't get it? I mean *really*. Make an acting choice that involves the fantasy of blood and guts, even if the play happens to be a British drawing-room comedy. Real bloodshed need not appear nor do we want it to appear; it is the *probability* of it appearing that excites us. Besides, people in drawing-room comedies have tremendous needs, too.

Do Not Fear "I Don't Know!"

If you suddenly realize that you don't know what either your objective or your action is, look on this as a valuable rehearsal tool. Actors sometimes panic if they are dead-locked in confusion about what is motivating their character, not realizing that it might be possible their character does not know what to do *either*. A lot is possible in the phrase "I don't know." If you truly do not know what you are doing you are free to do *anything*, without social more or protocol, no filter, no boundary, nothing to hold you back. Of course I am speaking here about rehearsing your monologue or scene; when performance comes you naturally must be – or at least *seem* to be – in complete control. But how marvelous to get there through the process of considering every conceivable idea in search of a solution! Think of all the off-beat, wrong and crazy ways you might approach a scene and you might create a performance that is genuinely different from the way the part has been played before. Your work can be truly 'in the moment' and it can mean that *anything* can happen. The audience will feel this, too. Take advantage of the "I don't know!" moments. Just remember to do such experimenting in rehearsal where you can apprise your partner of what you are doing. It is not professional to just spring it on them without warning during a show.

'Over the Top' and Doing 'Too Much'

The short answer to the question "Am I going over the top or doing too much?" is it *depends*. But for our purposes, since I want you to make more outrageous choices, I would like to suggest that for the most part there is no such thing as *over the top*. Whether in audition or performance an actor's loud, boisterous choices can only be measured and balanced relative to the quiet, honest moments they represent. Sometimes a character in an outrageous situation *has* to act in such a way that will cause an audience to think "That person is over the top." It is only when this occurs *all the time* that it can be said to be 'too much.'

As to the question of doing 'too much,' one of the biggest bones I have to pick with young actors is the question of making the 'big choice.' A play is about unreality; as long as you are true to the play you are acting in it is not likely you will drift over the top. When rehearsing, if you fear that you might be doing too much ask your director, or better yet tighten up your motivation – as a matter of fact if you have been overdoing the director will probably come to you *first*. Doing too much is probably because you don't know what you are saying or why. It *is* possible to do more than can be *believed* in a scene, given the style of the play that the director and playwright have established. That has nothing to do with being 'over the top' or 'doing too much.' After all, the actor's task is also to make the *un*believable *believable*.

Try this little test: put yourself in place of the audience or auditors. If you are moved to ask "Why are they doing *that?*" you are probably over the top or doing too much. Or worse: not doing *enough* to sufficiently motivate the genuinely outrageous choice that is required.

Playing Emotion

Emotion is at the heart of the actor's work. Be careful of too much of it, though. All an audience asks to see is a person who is doing the best they can. If you present this to us we will be with you. It is better if the performer gets only to the *precipice* of tears, not crying their eyes out. Acting is not therapy; it is self-indulgent to wallow in emotion as if you were on a therapist's couch. People do not want to cry; they want to *avoid* crying. But it overtakes them. Do you want to see a wimp who blubbers at the drop of a hat? Even though there are speeches that might require the character to get emotional and approach the verge of tears, the scene itself is about much more than that. The scene is also about the fight for one's heart's desire, yet to be resolved, from which the audience will hopefully glean some great truth about their own lives. Try fighting *against* the tears that want to come; if weeping happens as a result of this anyway, that's okay. In spite of all the times I have harped on making outrageous choices this is one case where moderation and economy will work best. If you weep once, we are moved; if you cry all the time we don't care and are bored by you.

Explode or Lose It?

A character may at some point reach their wits' end, a point in time when they just can't take it anymore and – 'blow up.' A blow-up or explosion in your monologue is good dramatically as well as dynamically, and is probably already built into the script by the playwright. That may even be why you picked the monologue in the first place, to show off your innate fire and, yes, even danger, as an actor. The difference between exploding and losing it is that an explosion is sudden, unplanned, maybe embarrassing and quickly followed by an apology. Losing it is much more far-reaching and potentially dangerous (only in the scene) because personal harm to the one who loses it or to those around him or her is a distinct possibility. This is the same for either dramatic or comedic monologues. Once you have found such a moment in your speech, however, look also for the point when the character is striving to *calm down*. When it comes to exploding or losing it, these additional thoughts might be of use.

1. Unless the script calls for otherwise, try to explode only *once*. Save it for the right textual moment so that you aren't doing it the entire time.

2. You lashed out because of pent-up frustration *inside* you that finally boiled over, and there are many ways, physical as well as vocal, to display this. How about a SILENT explosion? How about one great unintelligible burst of SOUND without words before you continue on with your speech? Many more are possible, only limited by your imagination. Anything is possible in an outrageous situation caused by love.

3. Play the 'calm down' as trying to *recover* after your explosion. Think of yourself in real life: if you have just yelled at some-one, are you not nearly breathless? Is not your heart beating rapidly? Do you not require a moment – perhaps even longer than that – to calm down? How we react *after* a great show of emotion can be more interesting than the outpouring of that emotion in the first place. Some of the many active verbs that might be possible to play include to catch (your breath), to gulp (for fresh air), to plead or beg (for forgiveness).

4. See what happens to you after you have just blown up. Nobody wants to be harsh or rude to people, to shout at them, even when events force us to it. Even if we bark at someone we do not like – versus shouting out of frustration linked to love – most of the time we are not happy with ourselves later, not happy with our *failure*. In those seconds after the blow we go through a lot of things, think a lot of things *and feel* a lot things before we are moved to finally say "I'm sorry I yelled ...." As an actor pay close attention to what is happening to you every single moment. You might be pleased to find out what is hap-pening to the roomful of people you have just auditioned for, as well.

Realism Is Not Real

Even in the sparest iterations of Realism a theatrical event is not real, nor was it ever meant to be. Then it would cease to be Theatre. After all, we can see that the actors are in makeup and costume, that they are moving about arbitrarily under hot lights on a stage; we might even be able to see the sweat glowing on their foreheads and watch how high the spit flies as they project their lines. We accept that they are in that Victorian drawing room or Tower of London or Forest of Arden or deck of the Titanic. What makes stage acting special is the fact that you can never allow yourself to completely lose control – *that* is part of the magic, as well; otherwise someone is going to get hurt. Would you do a sword fight with an actor so 'into it' they have lost control? That's why scenes with stage combat or dance combinations or anything potentially dangerous are always rehearsed before the show each night, and why the actors doing the combat (especially the ones who are supposed to suffer the most damage) hold fast to eye contact during that scene in the play. For all of the honesty and 'realism' sought for in the theatre, it is, after all, only an *illusion*, a lie like truth, as Macbeth says. The stage asks the actor to live in two universes: one in which they really seem to *be* the character they are portraying, and the other in which they are technically vigilant about remembering their lines and their blocking and being in proper light and careful not to accidentally kill someone while wielding a plastic sword. It is quite a challenge, which is why stage acting remains one of the true tests of an actor's metal.

Acting onstage you are always being watched and listened to, and your acting choices must accommodate this, whatever adjustment might have to be made to compromise 'realism' with 'theatrical.' Naturally you want to make choices that are believable. In addition, as you work keep your choices in the realm of the *observable*, so that the paying customers can get the story. Don't fall in love with being *real* onstage; fall in love with *being* onstage.

But I Can't Do It *That* Way because My Line Says *This!*

"I love you" doesn't have to be said 'lovingly' any more than "I hate you" has to be said hatefully. This is what is known as *irony.* You are in rehearsal, right? Even though the playwright may have written a line with the intention of your character speaking it in a certain way, how about seeing what happens if you try something outrageous? Play an argument as a love scene and a love scene as a knock-down, drag-out fight. Or better yet, experiment with playing every *other* line with its opposite meaning. Who knows? You just might make an exciting discovery.

Your *Acting* Makes Dialogue Realistic

Words the playwright has given you to speak don't need to be realistic. They are there to help him or her tell the story of their play, and if the play is worth doing it is because the playwright has listened to *their* ear, not yours. Those words came out of their psyche and imagination, and though they might have been suggested by their own experience they are still not real life. Naturally you might first think of this when trying to make Shakespeare and other classical plays sound realistic, but contemporary plays can also be tough going. Consider the Sid monologue we pieced together from Clifford Odets' *Waiting for Lefty.* In his work, Odets created a style of language all his own. Most of his plays were written at a completely different time in America, during the Great Depression, and his characters all speak in a 1930s street-wise, fast-talking, even *poetic* vernacular, which at first might sound corny to the ear of an actor today. The way to address this is, as always, to concentrate on playing the *needs* of the character in an outrageous situation, perhaps even more outrageous because the character is moved to use what might sound like overly colloquial language. I even had a young student once struggle like crazy trying to motivate the word "Golly!" As an actor you make the playwright's words 'ring true' in the ear of the audience by fighting for the human desire that prompted those words.

That is what makes them 'realistic' as well as 'believable.' The actor can't complain "That's a hard line to say!" No. It is a line spoken out of tremendous need, which is perhaps never easy to be said, yet *must* be said.

Meet the Play on *Its* Terms

Sometimes when actors work on a pre-twentieth-century period piece, such as *Lady Windermere's Fan* or *Miss Julie* or *Mrs. Warren's Profession*, etc., they forget that it has been written in a time, place and culture far removed from our own. Rightfully they play actions to win objectives and they recognize that those characters are imperfect, flesh and blood, just like them. Unfortunately it is then that value judgments of the New Millennium sometimes creep in. They might shout "Why would I do that?" or "I would never do that!" or even "What a stupid thing to do!" In approaching these plays you are not only bound to do what that playwright has written for you to do; it's also important to accept that they might be of a cultural paradigm that motivates them in entirely different ways than you might expect. This is where research comes in. These characters act the way they do because of the *society* in which they lived and *hoped to thrive*. Hence in Chekhov's *Three Sisters*, Toozenbach allows himself to be goaded into a duel with pistols. Hedda Gabler is driven to suicide in preference to what, for her, would have been worse than death: public scandal. Despite our rightful insistence on women being able to control their own lives Kate submits herself to her husband Petruchio in *The Taming of the Shrew*, and Othello kills Desdemona out of preserving his honor thinking it a sacrifice – though sadly we see real-life events echo these scenes very similar actions today. In societies before the twentieth century people wore tighter, more constricting clothing (to make it that much harder to take those clothes *off* in sudden fits of lust, perhaps), and it might seem to us that their social views were equally as confining. Just the same, along with trying to come up with exciting active verbs to describe their action or name their objective actors also must make the effort to remember – and study – the kind of play they are acting in.

Rehearsal Clothes Help You Play Period Style

In classical period plays knowing what you will be wearing will help you work on the physicality of your character. Unless the design has been updated to be contemporary, specific movement and gesture will be required to portray people of previous centuries, relative to the social mores they lived under and sought to thrive in, and adjustments to what you might wear in rehearsal can get you thinking and moving like your character almost right away. A tighter collar, a hoop/rehearsal skirt, corset, waistcoat, hard-sole shoes, suit jacket will all help you get started (versus torn blue jeans, ripped T-shirt and sneakers). The costume designer will certainly be able to provide you with this clothing or costume pieces to replicate it. In the rare case that they might not – for budget reasons, perhaps – try to find something you can wear to do this on your own. It is also a good idea in rehearsal to attempt to approximate your character's dress no matter what the period; it will save you time getting over that sudden restricted feeling actors sometimes get when in costume for the first time at dress rehearsal.

Roll Up Your Sleeves!

And speaking about clothing for rehearsal, I just have to mention a pet peeve of mine. It may never have occurred to you but look out for it from now on. Sometimes rehearsal halls can get cold and drafty and it can cause the actor to want to put on a sweater. This is fine. What I would like for the actor to avoid however is allowing their sleeve cuffs to *droop down over their hands*, so that they look like Bob Cratchit wearing fingerless gloves! Humor me here. Admittedly something like this – your sleeves dangling over your hands – might seem minuscule and harmless, but think of how it can affect your acting. The drooping fabric tends to make the actor's fingers curl up like claws, shrinking their hands into their sleeves so that gestures with the fingers, hands and arms get timid and recede back, resulting in movement that is not nearly as specific and strong as it might have been. See what I'm talking about? Both men and women have been guilty of this but I have to say that I have mostly observed ladies doing this. Roll up your sleeves before you work a scene so that you will have a full range of motion! If you are cold in the studio do some jumping jacks before you get started!

And both sexes: roll up the cuffs of your *jeans!* Unless you are playing a vagabond ratty, wrinkled pants-cuffs falling over your sneakers aren't going to help you become Henry Higgins or Eliza Doolittle in *My Fair Lady!*

13

PERFORMANCE NOTES

There Is Never a Fourth Wall

This is not the most earth-shaking note in the world but I want to mention it because it can cause actors to make choices that are not as big or risky as they might be. Sometimes when performing in a realistic play on a proscenium stage actors allow the conceit of the 'fourth wall' to limit their performance to the confines of the stage alone, as if they have lost all awareness that people are out there in the auditorium watching. This is out of striving to sustain the 'realism' of the modern play they are in and that is good, but actors should not forget that they are telling a story to an audience and must *share* it with that audience. I have seen this several times when viewing a play and it always makes me want to shout "Hello! We're out here! Don't forget about us!" Realize that onstage you are always exposed, you are always seen by at least someone or presenting 'back' to them, and not just because the stage has been configured into the shape of a thrust or round or because the blocking has you moving in a certain direction. By 'sharing' the play I do not mean that you should break the fourth-wall illusion and start talking directly to the audience when it is not called for in the script. I am only suggesting that even in the most realistic of plays it is still necessary, aesthetically as well as technically, to *engage* the people out there viewing the performance. You can accomplish this by making choices that create greater desire in the heart of your character and also by simply 'cheating out.' Doing this is also a great way to stay 'alive' onstage, always listening and 'in the scene.' The challenge and the glory of stage acting are that you and the audience are entering into a two- to three-hour contract based on what Samuel Taylor Coleridge called the "willing suspension of disbelief." Both of you know full well that the play being performed that evening is not real and not meant to be real, yet you *accept it* as real. Because of this it can be argued that there is never really a 'fourth wall,' even in the most naturalistic of plays. This sets stage acting apart from the other acting mediums and is what makes it truly out of the ordinary – that is, makes it *outrageous.*

Hold for Laughter

Even though you hold for laughter after a funny punch line in a comedy you are not ceasing to be in the play. During those seconds that you are waiting for the crest of the laugh to start downward – which is when you speak again – you should still be reacting, still in the world of the play. We accept the stage convention that you are pausing to allow the audience time to enjoy their laugh. As you wait for audience laughter to rise and then fall you can pretend that your character is so deeply caught up in the moment that you had to take a 'breather.'

In the Moment

You have to be ready for whatever happens, unplanned, during your monologue or scene; that is, you always need to be *in the moment.* Being in the moment will make it possible for you to react based not on what you might have rehearsed but on what has just happened organically in the scene; and to do this you will have to be honestly listening and registering what has actually been said to you. It does not serve your performance to memorize every single reaction; that only makes you an acting robot that is not really living in the play. (And by reaction I am not talking about what the stage directions say you do;

naturally you will commit those to memory. I am talking about your unique acting choices based on moment-to-moment playing with your scene partner.) What should be memorized are your words, your relationship to the people around you and what you want from them. Once this is understood there is a lot of freedom in how you actually accomplish those objectives. During a scene sometimes wonderful unplanned things can occur and you want to avoid being caught 'glassy-eyed,' having effectively dropped out just because you do not have lines. One of the most difficult roles of this type to play is the Shakespearean servant – or actually *any* servant. With these roles you are either placed in the position of having to stand there silent (and actively listening) for long periods of time or – and this is the greatest challenge – after having been offstage for a long time you make an entrance having to deliver lines of earth-shattering consequence, such as when Seyton says in *Macbeth:* "The queen, my lord, is dead." I know. I played Seyton.

Playing Crowd Noise

I mention this because at the beginning of your career it is very likely that you will be in a lot of crowd scenes and called upon to make 'crowd noise.' The first summer of my own career I acted with a Shakespeare festival in a production of *The Comedy of Errors* with an old-fashioned, declaiming-type actor. His technique was based on using the power of his voice – which was substantial – as a means to show nuance and emotion in his performances. In the final revelation scene in *Errors* the cast onstage was directed to make a great deal of crowd noise of shock at what was happening – what theatre people used to say could be accomplished by the actors muttering "peas and carrots" over and over under their breath. I was near this older actor and so we were directed to play the moment to one another. When I turned to look at him I saw that his eyes were glassy, empty, bulging wide-open, and he was mouthing *gibberish* to me, like "Ooba Doobah! Aaabadabbah! Eeebee deebeeh …!" He did not even attempt to engage me honestly; he did not really even *see* me, even though he might have appeared to be 'looking' at me.

The elder actor's acting style aside it may be that some of the reason behind his choice was that he was not comfortable ad-libbing Shakespeare (or ad-libbing in general). Nowadays we look on crowd noise a little differently and can accept that it comes out of the dramatic needs of the moment, and this allows the actors to actually speak real words to each other. What I have done, and what most directors do when dealing with a scene requiring improvised crowd noise in a Shakespeare play, is to simply pick words and phrases from the play itself that can be thrown in during the scene of loud confusion and hubbub: "Alas!," "It's possible?," "Is't so?," "God's blood" or "'S'plood!," or calling the affected characters by name: "Benedick?," "Beatrice?" and repeating aloud what has just happened to them, such as "In love?," "Dead?," "Gone?," etc. The actors can then play the scene full-throated without fear of not knowing what to say. It is the director's job to listen for errant contemporary exclamations that might slip out as well (such as "Golly gee!," "Get outta here!" or "Holy S—T!"), but as the actor onstage you should be aware of it, too.

Don't Look Down for Too Long – Even into a Grave

Actors in the Requiem in *Death of a Salesman* are gathered at the gravesite of Willy Loman, gazing down at his grave wondering what made him kill himself. Even though that is what is going on in this final scene, the audience still wants to see the actors' faces so they can hear and understand what the characters, speaking softly because of the intimacy of the moment, are saying. It is true that it is the director's job to insure that performers are positioned in such a way that they can be seen and heard properly, but actors ought to be aware of their surroundings in this regard as well. What will help all of this is if the actors *cheat up* as much as they can, even though their concentration and emotion is focused down toward the floor. Think of playing the scene with the characters gazing up as they remember the *past* and consider the *future*: a past that is *outside of them* and a future that is *just ahead* of them. The audience will still believe you are at a gravesite.

Let the Audience Do the Feeling

Sometimes actors feel the need to 'help the audience along' when the play gets emotional. They may even try to feign a few sniffles, or tears. Whether actors in doing so realize it or not, this exposes a desire on their part to be *loved* by the audience by getting them to feel sorry for them. I am not against paying customers liking a character, although being likable is not necessarily what performers are up there for. Emotional moments might engage your character in roughly the same way that you yourself would be engaged at that moment; grief and mourning can be expressed in a lot of ways, not just through the wailing or gnashing of teeth. For most of us it's likely that the instinct will be to 'keep it together' as best we can instead of getting completely swept away by emotion. Continue to fight for what you want in the scene and let the chips fall where they may; if emotion comes to you and you fight it even more emotion might come. That is what humans are like. On the other hand if in a play you feel the need to *show* the audience how emotional you can get, then it may be you are playing a different objective entirely ...

Stage Whisper

Try to avoid actually whispering. It is bad for your throat. Think of a 'stage whisper' as *the desire to keep from being overheard.* This will allow you to actually speak with your full voice – the audience will accept this theatrical convention – and you will still be *believed* to be taking someone aside to share a confidence. That is probably why it is called a '*stage* whisper.'

Always Finish the Un-finished Line

Go through your script and find where your character's line ends in an ellipsis (...) or a dash —. In some cases, such as the dash, your scene partner will probably be the one to stop you, and in others, as with the ellipsis, you probably are meant to drift off because of some sudden thought. Try to imagine what your response *might have been* had you not been interrupted and pencil it into your script. As you rehearse the scene, speak this created line at the end of your scripted line, or at least *attempt* to. In the case of the ellipsis – where you are meant to trail off – play the moment as a conscious effort to *avoid* saying what you would have said. In the case of the dash keep talking until your partner stops you; *make* them stop you. Often actors will anticipate being interrupted. This can make for a herky-jerky rhythm in the scene and creates the habit of *expecting* to hear a certain line – or worse, certain line reading. Always keep talking when the scene has you in a false stop – yes, go ahead and make up the words. Your scene partner will cut you off. Perhaps you will end up overlapping your partner (you can apologize to them later), which will keep the scene moving and perhaps drive you to even more outrageous choices.

The Exit Line

If you have a false exit – your attempt to leave the room is interrupted when another character calls you back, stopping you short – *keep walking.* Your objective is to get out the door because whatever it is that caused you to want to leave is still driving you. Don't anticipate being prevented from going and don't walk *just slowly enough* for your scene partner to be able to catch up with you. *Make* them stop you from leaving!

Also always hit the exit line a little harder. Because you are going out the door, most likely upstage, the audience may lose sight of your face and hence your words. The exit line is often of great importance, whether for plot (think of Hamlet's "The play's the thing / Wherein I'll catch the conscience of the king!") or as a capper to the play ("On the contrary, Aunt Augusta, I've now realized for the first time in my life the vital Importance of Being Earnest."). Make sure the audience hears it clearly.

Play a Comedy like a Tragedy ...

"Play a comedy like a tragedy and a tragedy like a comedy."
This is an old saying; I don't know who said it first. But it's a
helpful little jingle. We laugh at the people of *The Importance of
Being Earnest* because they treat the most serious things in life
("And now to minor matters: are your parents living?") with
the most supreme triviality (The subtitle of *Earnest* is *A Trivial
Comedy for Serious People*). Conversely, we cry over Willy Loman
in *Death of a Salesman* because he took the most trivial things
("be well liked; it's not what you do but who you know") far too
seriously. When working on a comedy look first to how large
you can make your concern for the smallest things, the most
frivolous, meaningless things. Then play them as seriously as
if you were acting *Medea*. For tragedy find the opportunity to
laugh, even to be silly. The audience will welcome such levity.
You will also be enriching the play by unearthing its opposites.

Playing Age

Age-appropriate casting seems to be the fashion these days, and
this means the instance of young actors judiciously applying
grease-paint pencil marks to their face for wrinkles and painting
their hair with white shoe polish to play age is very rare. I am sad
to see this theatrical custom go; I want young actors in training
to experience every bit of magic the theatre has to offer. That
said, if by chance you do find yourself in the position of playing a character in, say, their sixties or seventies or even older,
know that one of the things that will age you most to the eye of
the audience is *economy of movement*. The elderly welcome still-
ness; they have lived a long life and are slowing down, having
fought all the battles, seen strife as well as joy and perhaps wish
to finally take a rest. Like Lear they are ready to confer their
problems and obligations "upon younger strengths while we /
Unburdened crawl toward death." The young are in constant
motion, shifting from left leg to right leg, waving their arms at
every vocal utterance, always finding something to fidget about,

their hair or nose or ears, as if they simply cannot stop moving. Consider the gesturing of your hands. You might be tempted to point with your finger three times when you realize you can cut it down to one; instead of flopping down into a chair with youthful abandon you discover it's better to lower yourself gradually as you sit down because you have gotten so heavy or feeble with age you might break a hip. Even as you are sitting still gestures of any kind should be sparing. It may be that at your advanced age you just don't have the energy to do any more than that. In my production of *Cat on a Hot Tin Roof* I cast a college senior who had only just turned 21 as Big Daddy. He was (and is) a fine young actor, and because of this he tended to overdo, particularly in waving his arms or jumping up to make sudden – and youthful – movements. What I hit upon was to tie him up with rope – yes, I'm serious – all around his torso, essentially locking his elbows to his sides so that he was forced to walk, sit down, get up and gesture with greater simplicity. It worked. The less he moved the more presence he had. You will be surprised how aged – and how *powerful* – you can look when doing something as simple as not moving at all.

One quick sidelight about this. Avoid the temptation to allow your vocal production, out of a desire to indicate advanced age, to slow down or become halting. Prevent this by prompt *cue pick-up*; if you come right in on every cue you might be able to take a little extra time *during* the line itself, but not before. The play still needs to move, even when old people are talking. The old age of a character in a play is as unreal as the 'stage whisper.' The 'crotchety old voice' is a stereotype. Old people talk the way they do because of a wide variety of health conditions and ailments. That is actually what makes for the "childish treble turning toward pipes and whistle" Shakespeare speaks of in *As You Like It*, and it can only be achieved in study, observation and rehearsal. But even the best rendition of an aging character's voice must still be projected to the back row of the theatre, just as loud and clear as the voice of the young whipper-snappers.

Acting with an Accent

Sometimes, if they have not had a lot of training, when actors appear in a play requiring a foreign accent the evening becomes more about them struggling to pronounce rehearsed pronunciations rather than about people living in the work-a-day world who *happen* to speak with an accent. In the case of the British accent, for instance, the audience can hear various odd and inconsistent sounds that gravitate wildly from Victorian England to the Mississippi Delta. The notion that these plays require a 'perfect' accent is mistaken. While it may be so for film it is not necessarily the case for theatre. If you have ever listened to the Jerry Blunt tapes of the Cockney accent, for example, you will realize at once that they are almost unintelligible to the American ear! And these examples are *perfect*. What is wrong? The problem is that for the stage you don't have to try to sound perfect; you only have to accurately create the *rhythm* and *sense* of the speech. Theatre is illusion and heightened reality; to be successful you only have to portray what *rings true to the ear of the audience*. They will hear what they *believe* to be a 'perfect' accent. In any event even the most proficient accent will need to be adjusted and adapted to the stage for simple understanding. All that really is necessary for the audience are those few more recognizable points of rhythm and pronunciation. My view is that when doing a British accent for theatre American actors only need to employ what is known as Standard American Stage Speech, established by the teaching of Edith Skinner, which to our ear today sounds British because it has the most familiar sounds, such as the back-of-the-throat 'a's and soft 'r's: *AAHH*-nt for aunt and c*AAH*-n't for can't, hea-*uh* for here and thea-*uh* for there. This technique frees you to fight for what the character *wants in the scene*. You don't have to worry that your performance will be thought fake because the accent has been selectively modified for the stage; that is how every performance of an accent is best approached. What actually makes performances seem fake is not honestly *playing the play*.

On the other hand, if you can produce an accent that is perfect and you can still be understood by an audience, great. Just remember that these plays, like all plays, are more about people trying to survive in *that* society than about how fluently they substitute diphthongal changes.

A word about the southern accent: if you are cast in a play by Tennessee Williams (or any southern writer) it is not necessary to push the twang. All that is needed is to fight for the objectives of a person who *happens* to have been born in the south. Concentrate on the southern affinity for telling a story, for the very hard lines drawn between masculinity and femininity, and particularly with Williams for seething sexual longing and repression. With his plays the only thing that really needs to be dealt with, frankly, is *sex*. If by chance your production is being done by a theatre company in the southeast, in my opinion you can tread even more lightly on the dialect, if attempting to do it at all. At my school for instance most of the students I have had are from the south, and as such their native speech is, at least rhythmically, already close to Williams' characters. It might be said that they know those people even if they don't know that they know them. I didn't have to lift a finger to coach the actors' accent in my production of *Cat on a Hot Tin Roof*. Whatever the role or genre, fight to overcome an outrageous situation caused by love, and you will be playing the roles believably enough.

Playing the Rich

In his 1924 short story "The Rich Boy" F. Scott Fitzgerald said "Let me tell you about the rich. They are different from you and me." I beg to differ. If we are referring to tremendous amounts of money, the best schools, the most opulent shelter, expensive clothing and luxurious food, then I am forced to admit yes, in these ways they are set apart. But notice that all of these things are *possessions*, which ultimately have very little to do with people who are sometimes caught up in outrageous situations caused by love. In this regard it can be argued the rich feel everything as profoundly as we poor folks do and they need everything we need. When doing these plays begin with what do these characters want out of life? You can always add stiff clothing, dialect and picking up the teacup with your pinky finger pointed skyward *later*.

Playing Royalty

In Shakespeare's *Henry V*, out of a desire to assure his French bride-to-be that it is quite all right for her to give him a kiss before they are married King Harry says "O Kate, nice customs curtsy to great kings. Dear Kate, you and I cannot be confin'd within the weak list of a country's fashion; we are the makers of manners, Kate." This is instructive for the actor when cast in the role of a king, queen or royalty in general. Actors some-times make the mistake of feeling they have to affect some kind of carriage or bearing to *prove* to the audience that they are 'royal.' Why not simply play the part as a human being who just *happens* to have been born into a royal family? There is no need to *indicate* the majesty; there are good kings and bad kings, tall kings and short kings, well-bred kings and ill-mannered kings. People who are royal have access to all the breeding the world can provide and yet they can be just as ill-mannered, slovenly and foul as the rest of us commoners. But we accept them as a king just the same because they *wear* the crown. They are people, too; even a king had to be *taught* how to walk wearing a crown. It is true that in some scenes it will be necessary for the king or queen to outwardly display the respect that they hold for their office; world leaders and dignitaries in this coun-try and all over the world understand that and play by those rules of etiquette. Underneath all that royal garb they are – and *should* be – just as screwed-up as the rest of us.

Playing a Hero when You're Supposed to be a Hero

My thoughts on this are similar to "Play a comedy like a tragedy and a tragedy like a comedy." Unless you are in a melodrama try to also play the opposites in a character, his or her complexity. Only in comic books are heroes and heroines flawless in word and deed; the audience is unimpressed by such characterizations. What moves us is when we see characters we can feel are like us – that is, who have faults, who mess up, who *fail*. In our eyes their ability to rise above their failure is what makes them *heroic*. When playing the great heroic roles seek the real humanity that can be found when you don't think of them as a 'hero' or 'heroine.' Play their weakness, their vulnerability: for St. Joan help us see a young country girl's *fear of death* at the stake; allow St. Thomas More to *question* his piety and faith; in *The Crucible* portray John Proctor's desperation to *preserve his good name,* even if it means execution. These are the acts of people *called* to heroism, not born to it, and we are moved to tears by them in part because we are not sure we could do the same thing if in their place.

14

DIRECTOR'S NOTES

"Pick It Up"

When a director asks you to "pick it up" they are not always asking you to go faster (though in some cases that is indeed what they want). 'Pick it up' is also about the director wanting you to fight harder for your objective. They wisely recognize that this expediency will give the actor the sound and *appearance* of going faster, which is a far more organic and un-self-conscious way to get the scene to move. Know of course that they have every right to more directly say "Go faster!"

Act *on* the Line

One of my favorite notes, among the oldest in theatre. This happens a lot with beginning actors. Upon hearing their cue, *before* they reply, they start pausing and scrunching up their face, going through all sorts of gyrations out of an attempt to react *before* they finally decide to speak. Doing this only slows down the play. Any reaction from you must come *at the same time* you are speaking your line. This will keep the play moving. Your director will be grateful to you for this, too.

Your Actual Cue in a Scene

Your cue to respond in a scene is not actually the last *word* of the person who has just spoken to you; it is prompted by something that is said by your scene partner *before* they have even finished talking, perhaps as far back as the middle of their line.

Example: someone says to you,

"Outside of making you look *fat*, that dress looks great on you."

What makes you want to respond is when you hear the word "*fat*," right? *That* is your 'cue,' not "you." The fact that it was followed up with "great" doesn't register with you because you are still thinking about having been called "fat." Look for these inciting words in your scenes. You don't have to interrupt the other actor with your line in response – although scenes are not harmed when actors are so anxious to reply they end up cutting each other off – you will still wait until they have finished. Simply listening and taking in the truth of what they have said *as they are still talking* will keep you on the brink of the impulse to speak, and this will keep the scene alive and on cue. It also has the acting benefit of making you react to what your scene partner *does* as well as to what they say. Their calling you "fat" is an *intention*. So too will you be playing an *action* with your reply. That's why we say act *on* your lines, not before them. This can also be done in monologues, where you are constantly reacting during your *own speech* to what your invisible scene partner has said!

Listening

Believe it or not it is possible, when you begin training as an actor, to forget how to *listen*. Yes. Actors get so consumed in working hard they can lose sight of the simplest, most ordinary daily activities, such as honestly just *listening* to what another person says to you. They begin to think that the act of listening has to be *acted* as well, when in reality the act of listening itself comes closest to the one passive thing an actor in a scene does – this is completely different from *hearing*, which is something else altogether and must always be active and driven and explosive because at that point you are *understanding* what your scene partner *means* by what they have just said.

Once again I speak of the older actor I appeared with in *Comedy of Errors* so long ago. As I say, his was a great, bass-baritone vocal instrument that was a pleasure to listen to; he had been renowned for it his entire career. The previous season he had won an award for his portrayal of Othello, and, not coincidentally, because of his acting style it seemed that all of his work seemed to be played like *Othello*: stately, grand, resonant. I was told that in preparing for a part he would put his lines on tape and try to divine the best way they *sounded*. He would do this without any rehearsal with another actor; he would simply set it down in his mind that a certain line had to be *read* a particular way. What this led to, of course, even though he had had a long career at the point when I met him and certainly needed no direction from a snot-nosed kid like me, was that in the rehearsal and playing of a play he would not really listen to another actor. He would only memorize their line cue and more importantly this led to his locking in on how they most often *said* it. Sometimes some of the more experienced, Equity actors would play tricks on him and change their reading – in reality just play the scene! – and he would get thrown and flustered and forget his line because he heard something different from what he had been anticipating. He had not really been in the scene with them; he had been only playing *at* them. If you do this over time you will stop listening to other actors and be ever in danger of 'going up' on your lines if they say a line in a way that you do not expect. Isn't this non-listening against the spirit of what theatre is all about? Should we not all be playing the play *together*? In rehearsal you only need to memorize what you *want* from another person, then supply yourself with a few carefully chosen active verbs to get started, and then let it all just happen. Over time you will *both* arrive at the best way to play the scene in the end. Wouldn't that be more fun?

Earning a Pause

If you pause all the time (and the play is not by Harold Pinter) it will lose meaning and slow the play down. This has been said countless times to actors and it bears repeating. A pause isn't about *not* speaking. During a scene between characters it is when you give the other person the chance to state their case – which you *hope* will be agreement; as soon as you find out that your first attempt failed you are then forced to scramble for another tactic to replace your 'best' one! A pause is active, not passive. A monologue keeps you talking because you discover while you are doing it that you have more grievances that must be addressed, but even then the millisecond of a pause – best called a *beat* during a monologue – can happen because you feel the need to let them talk but at once *change your mind.* Pausing willy-nilly, thinking you are giving a moment 'affect,' will only bring the scene to a crashing halt. If, however, you briskly pick up all of your cues – as any actor portraying a character fighting for their life in an outrageous, loving situation should – and then you suddenly pause *once*, it will have greater meaning.

"Less Is More"

Of the acting notes most often abused and misunderstood, few have been more glommed onto than "Less is more." Actors get hung up on this adage because they concentrate on doing 'less' while forgetting that 'less' is only required because the character was already doing *more*. Yet that 'more' is *still required*. Only out of excess do we pull back; only after we have snapped at people do we immediately retreat and attempt to apologize, feeling that we were wrongfully harsh. It is true that the actor cannot dishonestly chew the scenery for the entire play but it is also true that what makes 'less' necessary is doing more than necessary in the first place. When directors caution the actor to "Just be simple. Do less ... Just *talk* to us," I think what they really mean is be more *specific* about what you are fighting for. Two things that can prompt this note come to mind: first they have witnessed an actor who appears to not know what they want in the scene or what to do to get it; lack of specifics makes the actor clumsy with their hands and needlessly loud with their voice (thus in danger of losing it). As the actor refines and clarifies their objective and action these gestures will simplify, their voice will calm down and their focus can be properly directed toward their scene partner. Second, a director might ask the actor to "just talk" because the actor has not really been listening to what the other person was saying, causing their responses to be confusingly large or small, not believable given the tone of what the other actor has said to them.

You should not take it personally when you hear the word "less." In the end the real agenda is to be as clear as possible. You are not editing yourself or holding back; you are simply trying to find the best way to play your role. Doing otherwise will only make your work bland, and worst of all unclear.

"Just *Say* It"

A director will sometimes give you a note to "Just say it." This can drive actors crazy because they get the idea that their work is bad and they are a failure in the part. This is not the case. Most of the time you hear it when doing Shakespeare and other classical plays to help actors avoid over-loud declaiming, but the principle is the same for contemporary plays. Not unlike "Less is more," "Just say it" is about the director attempting to help the actor be more clear, which will likely cause their work to be more *simple*. Though the actor is more than willing to 'tear it up' and scream and shout in a scene, maybe quiet honesty will do the trick. In essence the director is calling a 'time out,' to bring all the actor's more generalized bombast down to just the words printed on the page. There is no need to 'act.' Just say "I love you" or "I hate you" or "I'm tired" or "I'm so happy" as they are written. Sometimes a line really *means what it says*. Once this is done in rehearsal, once the actor knows exactly what they are saying and why, they can then probably play the scene with greater complexity and expansiveness than before, no longer making it muddy with over-thinking. This is the real value of "Just say it."

Consonants and Ends of Words

Sustain the energy through the end of the line, because (1) your character's needs are so great that you keep on talking, and (2) it will be easier for the audience to hear and understand you. American actors are notorious for losing energy at the end of a line because we get lazy with the ends of words. What normally happens is we first bark out loud with a great burst of volume, at the *beginning* of the line, then because of poor breath control we run out of air by the end. The opposite is what really is required: in projecting you gain momentum, with an ever-so-slight upward inflection by the end of the line. This is accomplished by hitting the consonants: the 'D's, 'T's, 'B's, etc. Sharpness with the ends of words helps you to be understood onstage, even in contemporary plays that beg for so much realism the actors cannot resist mumbling. Make sure that you hit the consonants very hard, perhaps even harder than you think might be necessary. To you it may feel false or too big but to the audience you will honestly *sound* conversational. Small studio theatres can cause actors to fall into mumbling habits. Most black box spaces are not sound-proofed and this makes them surprisingly more challenging to project in than larger proscenium auditoriums. The other challenge is that actors, bless them, sometimes get fixated on 'realism' when performing in the black box. The venue is so 'intimate' they think they can be heard just whispering. They are mistaken.

How to Play the Nonsense Words

Shakespeare is credited with making up some 17,000 words. This happened because in the throes of creating great dramatic literature he came across characters who could not express themselves in quite the way he wanted them, so because the needs of his characters defied definition he decided to augment the burgeoning English language by twisting sounds, contracting known words and phrases, any way that he could concoct them, and this led to the creation of entirely new words. In some cases he just plain dreamed up weird sounds that seemed to *sound* right to express what his characters were struggling to communicate. Some of these came to be called 'nonsense' words, and sometimes they can confuse actors even in contemporary plays today. Take Jim's speech to Laura in *The Glass Menagerie*. He is trying his best to make her see how great the world is going to be in the distant future, and this leads him to make sounds of airplanes soaring through the sky, of imaginary fists pounding: impulsive sounds meant to express some great success. Actors approaching such a speech sometimes get squeamish; they get confused about how to 'handle' these words which are more about sounds than communication. The way to play them is to follow the character's *need* in speaking them; this will mean *over*-emphasizing them, hitting the sounds and rhythm of those sounds as hard as possible because they want to make the person they are speaking to understand what they are saying. Think of how you celebrate when your favorite sports team scores the point that wins the big game: *YAAAYY!*, you shout. Or when you bang your big toe against a door: *DAG-NABBIT!*, you growl. Though none of us knows where "dag-nabbit" came from you can be sure that it happened out of the need to express pain that was so sudden and excruciating the suffering person had no words to describe it. Think of other words spoken out of exasperation, such as "Fudge!" "Darn it!" "Shoot!" not to mention a few more dirty choices, all exploding out of our mouths in an unguarded moment. In a loving, fun way out of a desire to impress Laura Jim is doing this. This is how to play those pesky 'nonsense' words.

Cheat Out

Young actors are nice people. They believe that it is impolite if you do not look someone in the eye as you talk to them. Being onstage is different: especially if it is a proscenium stage. The audience wants, *needs* to see you in order to understand you. It will be necessary to 'cheat out,' to position yourself in such a way that you *appear* to be talking directly to the other person while your face can still be seen by the audience. It isn't necessary to look your scene partner in the face all of the time, as I have mentioned before. You can also consider cheating out as an acting intention as well as theatrically expedient; what you are saying is so great, so profound that the images contained in your words cause you to dream aloud even as you are speaking, even as you are reminiscing. You will be sharing the play with the audience, and onstage you need to be doing it at all times.

Commenting on a Role

Sometimes an actor will perform a moment or a speech as if to cajole the audience into feeling a certain way. This happens when they are trying to get the audience to like them. They feel that if they are seen to be obviously sad or emotional the audience will in turn feel empathy, perhaps even get a little teary-eyed. Or, if the character is supposed to be a hero, they might work a little harder at proving how *tough* their circumstance is so that the audience will think them 'heroic.' This is very similar to the old seventeenth-century-inspired practice of 'claptrap.' Claptrap is when an actor does something they know will make the audience applaud. It is not about honesty or believability; it is about getting people to like you. By your actions you are winking at them and saying "Aren't I clever? Isn't this a great performance?" This also happens when an actor pre-judges their character, feeling that character to be a loser or a bad person in some way. The actor then makes choices either to be consciously bad or to be clearly a failure, in this case not only because they want the audience to feel that way too and 'get it': *they* feel that way, themselves. Shame on them!

Your choice, first and foremost, is about telling your character's story to the best of your ability. Avoid the temptation to say "boy, what a screw-up," or "what a bad person" or "what a loser." Like you, your character is someone who has been thrown into an outrageous situation they don't know how to deal with. As long as you portray that, no matter what the 'character' of your character is, even if the audience doesn't love you they will almost certainly be pulling for you. If you are cast in the role your opinion ought to be that Ebenezer Scrooge is the nicest guy in the world!

A Role You Have Played Before

Years ago word was that if you had played a part before a director would not cast you, because they were afraid that you would be locked into the same interpretation you had the first time and unable to think of it in a new way. There is some evidence to support this; I was cast as Sam in *Master Harold … and the Boys* once because the actor who had been hired originally – who by the way had played the role three or four times before that – proved virtually undirectable as he wasn't open to looking at the part any other way. The director finally chose, after a week of rehearsal, to fire him and I was brought in with two weeks of rehearsal left (also evidence that you're never out of the running for a role until the play *opens!*). This glorious turn of events aside (glorious for me, of course!), I have to say that in my personal experience it has proven that most directors in the professional world are very happy if they can find an actor who has played a part before. You are saving them precious time during rehearsal to work on other important things rather than go through the teaching–learning process they would normally have to go through with an actor new to the role. They can think "Okay. The actor's got this. Great. I can work on some other stuff." If an actor plays their cards right they can work all the time, setting up a near cottage industry for themselves by repeating roles in plays that are being done a lot. I have seen directors do this too, traveling from theatre to theatre to re-mount plays they have directed before. This happened for a few years with certain August Wilson plays, with a couple of directors who had apparently gotten Wilson's 'blessing' as interpreters of his work always in demand. It happened a lot with *Fences*, for instance, and those directors would work again and again. It is not impossible that you might be a little pre-disposed to the way you played a role before, and it can present a problem for a director who is coming to the play fresh. Just keep alert and ever willing to play and be open to new things. New discoveries are always exciting. By doing this you increase your chances of being cast. Knowing the part frees you to explore because you know all of the given circumstances and may even still have the lines memorized. In a rehearsal process that always seems to be too short, the director is going to be very pleased to avoid starting with you from scratch.

'Doing Too Much' Is a Good Note

If you get a note from the director asking you to 'pull back' or 'tone it down' take this as a good sign. Most likely it means that you are doing exactly what the director wants you to do; you are *working*, bringing to the table choices, ideas, imagination and yes, even talent. All of the choices are not going to be successful but at least you are bringing them in to try. It may even turn out that the director is not asking you to tone down or pull back as much as asking you to make more *precise* the great big choices you have already brought in!

When You Don't Get a Note, That's Good, Too

During notes after tech rehearsal the director has a lot of detail to get through. He or she has to give notes first to the lighting designer, costume designer, set designer and crew. Sometimes these notes will need to be worked on to clear up what might have gone wrong during the run. When finally free to join their actors directors will naturally want to get them out of the theatre to go home and rest as quickly as possible. The better shape the show is in the fewer notes the director will take. They won't give notes on scenes that are going well. Sometimes young actors get nervous if they are not mentioned during note sessions. They are like baby birds fearful of being pushed out of the nest to learn to fly on their own. They have probably been told they are doing good work already, but they can't help wanting to be reassured and stroked for a little longer before they have to jump out of the nest on opening night. At this late stage a director will not give you a note if they don't have to. The director is tired and wants to go home, too; it's not possible to hold hands with their actors forever. Don't think a director doesn't like your work if they suddenly stop coaching you close to opening. At this point a director only wants to deal with problems, nothing else. Actors, calm down! If the director has already told you that you are good and says nothing after that it means they're happy with what you're doing and you're good to go!

Don't Get the Same Note *Twice*

On the other hand, actors, do your job too and *write down* individual notes as you get them each night! I can tell you from experience that a busy director finds it *very* tiresome if forced to give an actor the *same note more than once!* It makes them think you aren't listening and are just blowing them off. Don't think you will be able to just 'remember' what the director said without writing your notes down. Actors: at every rehearsal bring your script, pencil and paper – or yes, now even your cell phone or tablet! – to write notes down. Take down what your director says and incorporate it at the very next rehearsal, making the points of nuance your own. Do your job, darn it!

"Louder, Faster, Funnier"

At its core this old theatrical joke is a pretty good note for the actor. You may have already heard it during notes after a run-through, whether it is a musical or a straight play. It has also become an adjectival phrase to describe the business of acting. It's quite simple: make sure that you are heard clearly, pick up your cues and raise the stakes as high as possible. This will work for tragedy, comedy and musical comedy. As a matter of fact, doing all of these three things consistently will make you more professional, as well.

15

TALENT

I cannot resist the urge to say a word about talent. In my view the question of whether or not you have talent is, as Hamlet would have said, where "madness lies." I have not spoken about talent before now because I simply feel it is less important than any of the other things I have talked about. Yes – *any* of the other things. In speaking to you it is my assumption that you have talent – or at least you *think* you do. Though talent is a wonderful thing you will find if you continue in the 'biz' that it is not the most important thing – at least not immediately. Bear with me here; at the end of the day I do believe that to succeed an actor must have talent. It *is* important, but there are so many variables in the process of acting, so many things that can get in the way even before you have been able to get up onto a stage to show the directors what you can do, that nobody can define it and almost no two people can agree upon it. It is *ephemeral.* Yet the question drives young aspiring actors to distraction and tears every day.

I think any young performer will be served best by simply working like the devil on what they can control – training in speech, singing, movement, text analysis, and most importantly *self-acceptance and self-love.* If you press me I will have to come down on the side of being *right* for a role as more important than being talented. I say this because directors, when viewing actors in audition, first concern themselves with "Is this actor right for the role I am casting?" If they decide the actor is right they can then ask themselves "Are they *talented* enough to play the part?" If that question can be answered in the affirmative, then you get the job.

But here is something else to consider. An actor can be so right that the director – in their director's *hubris* – thinks "I can work with this actor. I can *coach* them through the role." The value of Type is that crucial. On the other hand it is entirely possible that a director will say "Even though this actor isn't quite the right Type they are so good that I simply have to use them. I must have them in my show!" This is what you are hoping for every time you audition; that your talent will override the director's notion of the kind of actor they need to play the part. In fact, this is the age-old plea of every actor who enters the profession: "Just give me a chance and I'll prove to you how good I am!" Which is why I keep singing the praises of outrageous choices in your work, because I believe they will make your audition more persuasive thanks to your fearlessness.

So what then can we finally say about talent? What is 'Good?' What is 'Bad?' Who should be the judge of whether you are a good actor or a bad actor? The simplest answer to this question is *you* should be. Therefore let me ask you: if you were told that you were "not any good," would that stop you? Should you let it stop you? Would it not ultimately *empower* the actor who is willing to say "All right; so what if I am not any good as an actor? I am still bound and determined to HAVE A CAREER as an actor!" What could be more liberating? I'm not saying *you* aren't any good; we are only supposing here. The key is being able to accept the possibility of being *un*-talented so that you can be free to actually *BE* talented!

I admit this idea may take some getting used to. After all that I have said, in the final analysis talent remains vitally important if you are going to succeed in theatre. But if you really want to gauge how likely you are to have a career as an actor, probably the most reliable thing to look at is your *casting*. To be candid, no amount of determination is going to help you if you are never cast. If an assessment of your potential for success is possible this may be it – maybe not in the role you want or think you ought to have, but getting into a play *somehow.* If this does not materialize for you over time, if it seems you are never hired to play even the smallest role, I would say then that the handwriting – if such handwriting exists – is on the wall. And even then such a factor is not fool-proof because the business is teeming with performers who at one time might have been given up as uncastable by their peers and, lo and behold, through years of perseverance and working their butt off and never giving up, they managed to put together a career. This is why it is so important to know and accept your Type. You never know what might be possible. So it is truly a waste of time to shed blood, sweat and tears obsessing over it.

In my humble opinion your time will be better spent if you get up after reading these words and get to work fighting for what you want in outrageous situations in *life* as well as in a play. The question of talent will take care of itself. Please, never again allow yourself to sit cowering in fear of what a teacher – or some dumb *writer* – might say after you have asked them "Am I any good?" Instead I want you to ask them "Am I working *hard* enough?"

Then you might have a chance, because everything, or at least *almost* everything, will be for once in your complete control.

Summary of "Just a Few Notes for You"

1. Think "Up Good, Down Bad" to keep audition focus.
2. Don't hide or rush.
3. Don't try to be funny.
4. Make every choice visceral, about blood and guts.
5. Make positive rather than negative choices.
6. Realism is not real.
7. Rehearsal clothes help you play style in a play.
8. Holding for a laugh onstage still requires you to stay in the moment.

9. A stage whisper is about intention.
10. With an exit line make them stop you.
11. A stage accent must be adapted for understandability.
12. Play the upper class and royalty as human beings like yourself.
13. Play a hero as a normal person, not someone heroic.
14. "Louder, faster, funnier" is about being professional.
15. Don't dwell on the question "Am I talented?"
16. Concentrate on training, perseverance and love of self rather than talent.

EPILOGUE

In dreaming,
The clouds methought would open, and show riches
Ready to drop upon me; that, when I waked,
I cried to dream again.

The Tempest

Many years ago I appeared in a production of *Anything Goes* in summer stock. I played the role of The Drunk, which was a created character in the chorus. Because of my two left feet I was mercifully relegated to the back row of tappers during numbers requiring time steps ('faking it,' as it is called). Mostly I staggered onstage dazed from time to time and then finally exited. On closing night during the final scene, with the entire cast onstage as all confusions were resolved and love interests blessed, it started to rain outside. The theatre was housed in a building with a tin roof. As the rain, which was torrential, came down harder it became more and more difficult for the actors onstage to hear one another. The racket drowned out the voices of our cast. Soon actors who were only feet from one another had to shout at the top of their voices to be heard. This went on for several moments, until the audience finally realized what was happening and started chuckling at our plight. In turn the actors onstage, too, all of us, understood what was making the audience laugh and we began to chuckle and laugh out loud ourselves. It was not long before the play ended with both audience and performers alike sharing a theatrical moment in time when *everybody*, every single soul on that stage and in that audience, could revel in the fact that we were experiencing a play and *knew* it was a play, and this joyous revelation made it possible for us to share the experience together! I never forgot it, and it remains one of the most prized moments of my theatrical life. Maybe I had sensed it before but this single moment stands out in my mind as an example of the power of live theatre: the power to move, to cheer, to instruct and even to bring people together.

It may have been then that I realized how outrageous – in the most giving and loving sense of the word – the theatre could be, and it is this realization that has kept me chasing after that feeling ever since, in one show or another, after one audition or another, and now trying to share this wonder with my students, one by one. If you love the theatre as I do I am happy to report that your efforts, while along the way you might lose a few as well as win a few, are going to be worth it. And if in fact it can be called outrageous to perform a sixty-second monologue to get a job as an actor, allow me to return to Shakespeare's play about star-crossed lovers. After sharing a first kiss – which they euphemistically call a *sin* – the two teenagers find it so wonderful they cannot resist repeating it. Romeo says "Give me my sin *again* ..."

Couldn't have said it better myself.

GLOSSARY

Above

Upstage of a person or set piece onstage.

Action

1. What happens during the course of a play, i.e., the 'dramatic action.'
2. What the individual actor performs in a scene in order to accomplish something, whether it is to get something from someone else or to make them do something.

Antagonist

A person or set of circumstances that stand in the way of the leading character in a play, preventing them from getting what they want.

Antithesis

1. In rhetoric, the direct opposite of one thing to another.
2. In acting, making choices that help the actor discover the opposite aspects of their character's desire, as a means to create richer, more interesting moments onstage and greater humanity in their character.

Beat

1. A pause of short duration. Such as when you say "Take a beat."
2. The distance between the end of one thought and the beginning of another; also, a character's change in tactics.

3. A unit of action used by directors and actors to separate moments in a scene. It can be as few as five or six lines, or simply stage directions without lines.

Below

Downstage of a person or set piece onstage.

Blocking

The movement of actors in a scene onstage to allow the audience to see them as well as to create an aesthetic picture. In addition it is designed to give the actor destination as a motivation for their movement.

Counter

Stepping to one side to allow a fellow actor to cross past in front of you in order to give them focus.

Downstage

An area on a proscenium stage moving toward the audience, away from the back wall of the stage.

Edith Skinner (?–1981)

Edith Skinner was a renowned voice coach known for her book *Speak with Distinction: The Classic Method to Speech on the Stage* (1942). She was considered the foremost teacher of good speech for the stage in North America, teaching at Carnegie Mellon University and the Julliard School.

Exposition

The imparting of important information about the characters and circumstances of a play, normally delivered in conversation between characters in the play's opening scenes.

Foreshadowing

When a playwright hints at something in the dialogue or action that is to happen later in the play.

Fourth Wall

On a proscenium stage the imaginary window into which the audience looks to see the characters, and the fourth 'wall' resulting from the four-cornered configuration of the 'box set' of the picture-frame stage through which the actors look to be seen in front of the audience.

Given Circumstances

Information about the characters supplied by the playwright not presented onstage because it would make the play's run time too long. For the actor, Given Circumstances are vital clues to motivate their character's actions.

'Go up'

When an actor forgets a line during a performance.

Intention

Related to the actor's task in the play but sometimes confused between what the actor does and what the actor wants. In practice it best fits as a synonym for the actor's objective.

Konstantin Stanislavski (1863–1938)

Famed Russian actor, director, producer, teacher and co-founder of the Moscow Art Theatre, Stanislavski is credited with establishing the method of Physical Actions, the foundation of modern training for the actor. Included in this philosophy is Emotional Memory, Relaxation, Concentration and the Magic If, a valuable tool still used today as a means to help actors imagine themselves as the character they play. In the 1950s, as adapted by equally famous acting teacher Lee Strasberg, Stanislavski's system came to be called "The Method," with disciples such as Marlon Brando, James Dean and Marilyn Monroe. Stanislavski's books on acting include *My Life in Art* (1924), *An Actor Prepares* (1936), *Building a Character* (1948) and *Creating a Role* (1961).

Objective

What the actor wants from scene to scene and possibly from moment to moment in a play. Also referred to as intention.

Obstacle

Internal and external forces of the play that complicate the character's pursuit of their objective. These are normally events and plot complications. They can be set in motion by the antagonist.

Protagonist

The character about whom the play is written. Not necessarily the hero, the protagonist is simply the lead character whose fortunes are followed throughout the story of the play.

Proscenium

The 'picture frame' configuration of a theatre space in which the audience is seated in an auditorium at one end viewing the actors onstage at the other end. It is understood that they are 'looking in' on the characters of the play. The proscenium stage is also called a 'box set.'

Realism

What we accept as predictable reality of people, places and things in the world in which we live. In theatre it is the replication as closely as possible of the daily aspects of human life.

Subtext

True meaning that is hidden underneath a character's words rather than being stated aloud.

Type

1. The category an actor fits, determined first by their physical appearance and second by their acting ability. Such as 'young lover,' 'leading man/woman' or 'character man/woman.'
2. The form of this term as a verb to describe the process of excluding performers from being considered for certain roles in plays or musicals; they are 'typed out' of roles because they are deemed not right for those parts.

Upstage
1. An area on a proscenium stage moving toward the back wall of the stage, away from the audience.
2. Positioning oneself above (upstage of) another actor so that they must turn their back to the audience to reply to you. An actor can also upstage themselves if they wander too far below (downstage) another actor, causing them to turn their own back to the audience to speak.

Appendix A

MONOLOGUE SUGGESTIONS

To get you started I have listed a few monologues you might try. Undoubtedly there are many not here that you will discover on your own. They are from great plays by great playwrights and they continue to stand the test of time, and of course they still exist in print so you will be able to get a copy of the entire script to read. I have not characterized them as either leading/character/ingénu(e)/man/woman; I simply list them as plays with good speeches you can consider – I want you to read the plays and decide for yourself. They all, however, will fit a young actor in a sixty-second audition. In addition I have cross-listed some roles (and you can do the same) because they can be played by actors of any ethnicity.

I would also like to add that trends come and go and it is possible that some of the choices listed here may one day wind up on the 'Overdone List' of audition monologues. If so, simply keep searching the canon of great American theatre literature; this list is as much about encouraging you to read and learn as finding a speech. I have been careful to list the play and the character, not a specific speech, so you might be able to piece together a good sixty-second monologue from a scene between characters that has not been done before because it is not obviously a monologue. In addition I have this thought: if you do it well and it shows you off to your best advantage you should go for it, regardless of what anyone else has said (this includes

me). These listings are about getting you started. After that it
will be much easier to keep digging and explore further. Good
hunting!

Playwright	Title	Role(s)
Men		
Jon Robin Baitz	*The Substance of Fire*	Martin
Michael Cristofer	*The Shadow Box*	Mark
Athol Fugard	*Hello and Goodbye*	Johnny
John Guare	*The House of Blue Leaves*	Ronnie
	Six Degrees of Separation	Rick
Howard Korder	*Boy's Life*	Phil, Don
Arthur Kopit	*Oh Dad, Poor Dad … So Sad*	Jonathan
David Auburn	*Proof*	Hal
Neil LaBute	*Reasons to be Pretty*	Kent, Greg
	Some Girl(s)	Guy
David Mamet	*American Buffalo*	Teach
	Race	Jack
Emily Mann	*Still Life*	Mark
Mark Medoff	*Children of a Lesser God*	James
Arthur Miller	*After the Fall*	Quentin
	All My Sons	Chris
	The Crucible	John Proctor
	Death of a Salesman	Biff
Peter Nichols	*A Day in the Death of Joe Egg*	Bri
Clifford Odets	*Waiting for Lefty*	Sid
Eugene O'Neill	*Ah! Wilderness*	Richard
	The Iceman Cometh	Hickey, Parritt
	Long Day's Journey into Night	Edmund, Jamie
	A Moon for the Misbegotten	Jamie
Don Petersen	*Does a Tiger Wear a Necktie?*	Bickham
Paul Rudnick	*I Hate Hamlet*	Andrew
Susan Sandler	*Crossing Delancey*	Sam
William Saroyan	*The Time of Your Life*	Harry, Joe
Peter Shaffer	*Amadeus*	Mozart
Larry Shue	*The Nerd*	Willum
Neil Simon	*Biloxi Blues*	Eugene
	Brighton Beach Memoirs	Eugene
John Steinbeck	*Of Mice and Men*	George
Tom Stoppard	*Rosencrantz and Guildenstern Are Dead*	Rosencrantz
Paula Vogel	*The Baltimore Waltz*	Carl
Kevin Wade	*Key Exchange*	Michael
Thornton Wilder	*The Matchmaker*	Cornelius
Tennessee Williams	*Cat on a Hot Tin Roof*	Brick, Gooper
	The Glass Menagerie	Tom, Jim
	The Night of the Iguana	Rev. T. Laurence Shannon
	Sweet Bird of Youth	Chance

Playwright	Title	Role(s)
Lanford Wilson	*Burn This*	Pale
	Talley's Folly	Talley

Women

Playwright	Title	Role(s)
Jean Anouilh	*The Lark*	St. Joan
David Auburn	*Proof*	Catherine, Claire
Alan Ball	*Five Women Wearing the Same Dress*	Mindy, Georgeanne
Lee Blessing	*Eleemosynary*	Echo, Artie
Ketti Frings	*Look Homeward, Angel*	Laura
Athol Fugard	*My Children! My Africa!*	Isabel
	The Road to Mecca	Elsa
Joanna M. Glass	*Play Memory*	Jean
A. R. Gurney, Jr.	*Another Antigone*	Judy
Lillian Hellman	*The Children's Hour*	Karen, Martha
Tina Howe	*Coastal Disturbances*	Holly
William Inge	*Bus Stop*	Cherie
	Come Back, Little Sheba	Lola
	A Loss of Roses	Lila
	Picnic	Rosemary
Neil LaBute	*Reasons to be Pretty*	Carly, Steph
	The Shape of Things	Evelyn
	Some Girl(s)	Bobbi, Tyler, Sam
Terrence McNally	*Bad Habits*	Dolly
David Mamet	*Oleanna*	Carol
Emily Mann	*Still Life*	Cheryl
Jane Martin	*Keely and Du*	Keely
William Mastrosimone	*The Woolgatherer*	Rosie
N. Richard Nash	*Echoes*	Tilda
Marsha Norman	*Getting Out*	Arlie
Eugene O'Neill	*Anna Christie*	Anna
John Pielmeier	*Agnes of God*	Agnes
David Rabe	*In the Boom Boom Room*	Susan, Chrissy
Elmer Rice	*Dream Girl*	Georgina
George Bernard Shaw	*Saint Joan*	Joan
Diana Son	*Stop Kiss*	Callie
Paula Vogel	*How I Learned to Drive*	Li'l Bit
Kevin Wade	*Key Exchange*	Lisa
Wendy Wasserstein	*The Heidi Chronicles*	Heidi
Tennessee Williams	*Cat on a Hot Tin Roof*	Maggie
	The Eccentricities of a Nightingale	Alma
	The Glass Menagerie	Amanda
	The Night of the Iguana	Maxine, Hannah
	A Streetcar Named Desire	Blanche, Stella
	Summer and Smoke	Alma
Lanford Wilson	*Ludlow Fair*	Agnes
	Redwood Curtain	Geri

Playwright	Title	Role(s)
African American Men		
Amiri Baraka	*Dutchman*	Clay
Athol Fugard	*Boesman and Lena*	Boesman
	A Lesson from Aloes	Steve
	"Master Harold" … and the Boys	Sam
	My Children! My Africa!	Mr. M, Thami
	Sizwe Banzi is Dead/The Island	Styles, Sizwe
Lorraine Hansberry	*A Raisin in the Sun*	Walter Lee
	The Sign in Sidney Brustein's Window	Alton
David Mamet	*Race*	Henry
Eugene O'Neill	*All God's Chillun Got Wings*	Jim
	The Emperor Jones	Brutus Jones
	The Iceman Cometh	Joe Mott
Suzan-Lori Parks	*Top Dog/Underdog*	Lincoln, Booth
Howard Sackler	*The Great White Hope*	Jack
Sam-Art Williams	*Home*	Cephus
August Wilson	*Fences*	Troy, Bono, Corey
	The Piano Lesson	Boy Willie, Lyman, Avery
George C. Wolfe	*The Color Museum*	Ensemble
African American Women		
Jean Anouilh	*The Lark*	St. Joan
Athol Fugard	*Boesman and Lena*	Lena
	Sorrows and Rejoicings	Marta, Rebecca
Lorraine Hansberry	*A Raisin in the Sun*	Lena, Ruth, Beneatha
David Mamet	*Race*	Susan
Lynn Nottage	*Ruined*	Mam Nadi, Sophie
Suzan-Lori Parks	*In the Blood*	Bully
George Bernard Shaw	*Saint Joan*	Joan
Samm-Art Williams	*Home*	Two
August Wilson	*Fences*	Rose
	The Piano Lesson	Berniece
George C. Wolfe	*The Color Museum*	Ensemble

Appendix B

WHERE TO FIND MONOLOGUES

You will of course find them by reading plays. Begin first by asking your teacher or acting coach if perhaps they have a copy of the play you're looking for (read and return it promptly!) or if they may know where you can get your hands on it. Then you can try to find them at your local university/college library, especially if they have a decent theatre department. Or you may have to do a bit of online digging. If you have a used/vintage bookstore in your town that is also a good place to look. You will certainly be able to find them online by mail order from the Drama Bookshop; Dramatists' Play Service; Samuel French, Inc.; BN.com; or Amazon. Amazon is a particularly good source as it provides used versions of the scripts which can be nicely cheap. Below are street and website addresses for some of these resources.

Monologue Resources on the Web

I have listed these websites because they do provide speeches from actual plays that you can read. Some of them have snuck in a few monologues that are not from scripts, but there are otherwise so many you will still be able to skip the ones that don't in favor of those that do. Also listed here is a site where you can find a long list of 'Overdone Monologues.'

Smith and Kraus Monologues

Smith and Kraus Monologues is a mobile app that contains access to some 3,800 monologues, with new monologues "added frequently." It is available from ITunes and the App Store.

http://theactorsworkshop.biz/monologues__scenes
http://www.actorpoint.com/monologue.html
http://www.ace-your-audition.com/free-monologues.html
http://stageagent.com/monologues/browse/comedic
http://stageagent.com/monologues

Bookstores

The Drama Book Shop
250 West 40th Street #1
New York, NY 10018
(212) 944-0595
www.dramabookshop.com

Dramatic Publishing
311 Washington Street
Woodstock, IL 60098–3308
1-800-448-7469
www.dramapublishing.com

Barnes and Noble
www.barnesandnoble.com

Play Publishers

Dramatist's Play Service
440 Park Avenue South #11
New York, NY 10016
(212) 683–8960 www.dramatists.com

Samuel French, Inc.
235 Park Avenue South

5th Floor
New York, NY 1003
(212) 866-598-8449
www.samuelfrench.com

Theatre Communications Group
http://www.tcg.org/publications/books/

Monologue Books

You can find speeches in the following fine books. Smith and Kraus Publishers are particularly devoted to monologues. They have many monologue books available, more than are listed here. All of them conveniently list the monologue, the title of the play it's from and a synopsis of the scene. Don't forget to read the entire play.

Aston, Zielger Irene. *The Ultimate Audition Book: 222 Comedy Monologues, 2 Minutes and Under*, Vol. IV. Lyme, NH: Smith and Kraus Publishers, 2005.

Karshner, Roger. *Neil Simon Monologues (Acting Edition)*. Rancho Mirage, CA: Dramaline Publications, 1996.

Milstein, Janet B. *The Ultimate Audition Book for Teens: 111 One-Minute Monologues*, Young Actor Series. Lyme, NH: Smith and Kraus Publishers, 2000.

Ratliff, Gerald Lee. *The Theatre Audition Book*. Colorado Springs: Meriwether Publishing, 1998.

Ratliff, Gerald Lee. *The Theatre Audition Book 2*. Colorado Springs: Meriwether Publishing, 2009.

Overdone Monologues

http://www.monologueaudition.com/ma_overdone-monologues.htm

Appendix C

UNIFIED AUDITIONS

National Unified Auditions

AUDITION TIME: **two 1-minute** monologues
  CONTACT: www.unifiedauditions.com
These auditions allow students to be seen by numerous BFA programs in university theatre and they are held every year in January and February at four different locations across the country.

Unified Professional Theatre Auditions (UPTA)

AUDITION TIME: **90 seconds** for a monologue and/or song
  CONTACT: www.upta.org
Held onstage at Playhouse on the Square in Memphis, Tennessee every year in February, UPTA has established a superlative reputation in theatre as a place for performers, both young and not-so-young, to come to be seen by companies looking to hire actor/singers for work year-round.

National Unified Auditions and Interviews (NUAIs)

AUDITION TIME: **2 minutes**
  CONTACT: http://www.urta.com/Auditions-and-Interviews/what-are-the-nuais.html

These auditions are held each winter in New York, Chicago and San Francisco. They are sponsored by the URTA, the nation's oldest and largest consortium of professional, graduate (MFA) theatre training programs and partnered professional theatre companies. URTA was established in 1969 to work toward the highest standards in theatre production and performance, and to help bring resident professional theatre to the university campus and its community.

Atlanta Unified Auditions

AUDITION TIME: **2 minutes** for a monologue and/or song
CONTACT: http://www.atlantaperforms.biz/index.php
Atlanta Coalition of Performing Arts (ACPA) is a non-profit alliance, and for fifteen years has sponsored the Atlanta Unified Auditions in March of each year, where actors can be seen by many theatre companies in the southeast, most of them based in Atlanta.

Southeastern Theatre Conference (SETC)

AUDITION TIME: **1 minute** for a monologue or **90 seconds** for a monologue and song
CONTACT: http://www.setc.org/setc-screenings
SETC hosts auditions for **Professional Acting Jobs**, **Graduate School Admissions** and **Undergraduate School Admissions** at the Annual Convention in the spring and **Professional Auditions** at our Fall Events. Each spring SETC hosts combined Spring Professional Auditions where actors can get summer, year-round and/or seasonal work at professional theatres from across the nation. The auditions are held each March as part of the SETC Annual Convention. These auditions are open to all adults, senior citizens and students over the age of 18. Actors who do not yet meet ALL qualifications to apply as a professional have an opportunity to secure a slot at the Spring Professional Auditions in March by attending and advancing

from an SETC Professional Screening Audition in one of the ten states within the southeastern region.

MidWest Theatre Auditions

AUDITION TIME: **90 seconds** for a monologue and/or song
  CONTACT: mwta@webster.edu
More than 600 actor/singers and design/tech/stage interviewees have the opportunity to be seen by some fifty theatre representatives during three days every year. Both Equity and non-Equity actors may audition.

Twin Cities Unified Theatre Auditions

AUDITION TIME: **2 minutes** for a monologue and/or song
  CONTACT: dana@climb.org
Sponsored by Climb Theatre every year during March on the campus of Concordia University in St. Paul, Minnesota. Theatres throughout the state of Minnesota attend, including the likes of Mixed Blood Theatre and The Guthrie.

StrawHat Auditions

AUDITION TIME: **90 seconds** for two monologues or for a monologue and song
  CONTACT: http://www.strawhat-auditions.com
StrawHat supports professional theatre and the careers of non-Equity performers and technical artists looking to develop their careers in theatre through the combined auditions event once a year in New York City. Three days of auditions are held with the opportunity for some 700+ performers seen by 30+ theatres and producers looking to hire actors. The auditions are open to non-Equity performers age 18 and older.

Broadwayworld.com

http://www.broadwayworld.com/nonequity.cfm#

At this site you can find nearly countless listings for upcoming auditions across the country. You can search by region: East, Central and West.

Theatermania.com

www.theatermania.com

Theatermania.com is a website rich in all things theatre, especially when and where to audition for training programs and jobs, as well as the latest information on the theatrical season On and Off Broadway and across the country.

Appendix D

HEADSHOT AND RÉSUMÉ PRODUCTION

Precision Photos
260 West 36th Street
New York, NY 10018
800-583-4077
www.precisionphotos.com

Precision provide reproduction of 8 × 10 headshots, postcards, business cards, model comp cards and showcase flyers, and have a résumé center. You can upload your own JPEG headshot image to their site online, design its look down to fonts for your name and the border around your picture, and can also print your submitted résumé on the back of the photo, which you can preview via high-resolution email. They will then mass-produce it to your specifications and mail you the hard copies. They also offer video production service enabling you to tape your audition online, which they will edit, emailing you the Flash video.

Modernage
555 Eighth Avenue #2002
New York, NY 10018
212-997-1800
www.modernage.com

Modernage has been in existence for sixty-five years. Among other services you can design your own headshot or post-card online and order as few as ten 8 × 10s, with discounts on re-orders.

Colorworks
55 West 39th Street Suite 706
New York, NY 10018
212-382-2825
www.colorworksnyc.com

Colorworks' specialties include re-touching and color correction. The company has been in business since 1976.

Prima Design Web
191 14th Street NW
Atlanta, GA 30318
404-355-7200
www.primaatlanta.com

Dirt Cheap Headshots
818-533-1950
dirtcheapheadshots@gmail.com
www.dirtcheapheadshots.com

Dirt Cheap says on its website that it offers "the most affordable headshot printing on the planet!" Services include real photo prints, no lithography, no set-up fee and always color-balanced. They provide Do-It-Yourself ordering with Live Preview and they do not store your file. Their store is totally online.

Appendix E

ACTOR'S RÉSUMÉ TEMPLATE

I thought it might be handy to supply an example of a simple actor's résumé. Below is a template fashioned out of mine, the style of which I have finally arrived at after some thirty-five years. I say arrived at because during the course of a career you will be constantly changing and re-arranging your résumé, finding bits and pieces of this and that style you might have seen on other actors' résumés and liked. It is best to keep it as simple and as readable as possible, without getting too busy with categories or too many roles (yes, you can put down too many!) that can clutter the page. Over time I have cut various things to make room for new credits and abandoned others because they were beginning to get old; for instance I no longer list my schooling. I am an actor of a certain age with a long career and list of credits behind me; if by my résumé and audition a director cannot tell that I have been trained and trained *well* I don't need to work for them. As you can see on the sample it will work well for you to feature your name at the very top, either flush to the left or center (where I personally like it). Following the line of vision you will then place your important phone number(s) to the left. Time was when you might include your mailing address as well but that can be penciled in after you know directly to whom your résumé will be going. Unfortunately it is necessary for women to be careful where they give out their phone numbers so it is helpful to list a cell phone number in place of home number (if they are separate). Years ago this was solved by having an answering service but those days are gone. To the right you can list your height and your hair and eye color, but unless you are a Falstaffian character actor trying to sell the fact that you are fat you won't want (and are not required) to list your weight. Below this you categorize your parts; you can say "THEATRE," or "STAGE WORK" (as I do), or even "REPRESENTATIVE ROLES." I have seen New York actors who work Off Broadway as well as in regional theatre list them as "In Town" and "Out of Town," which I used for a few years. If your emphasis is theatre you will present those credits first, with all other acting credits listed after. If you have done a Broadway show you will list "BROADWAY" at the very top, no matter how small the part was. If film is what you're going after you simply flip the listings. It is not necessary or advisable to put down everything you have done; pick and choose, and list only the best roles – those roles that represent the actor you're trying to get hired. I have heard (if you have that many) that it is advisable to list no more than twelve roles, but you can decide for yourself. Ultimately the number is only important if you begin to fill the page and have to start cutting. The point is you don't want it to look cluttered and hard to read. If you have done only three or four parts, make certain that everything on the page is centered and spaced well, and list them with pride. Next category below is your "TRAINING," or "EDUCATION." Like I said, I'm an old guy and my audition should show where I've been and what I've done, and besides, the days of my trying to strike up a conversation based on where I went to school are long gone. I do welcome it, though, if a director looks at a certain role I have played at a certain theatre; striking up a conversation as one working professional to another is always welcome. If you are just starting out, however, list your school, your major, the degree you earned and the years you were there. If instead of going to college you went to an acting studio for a

certificate list that. Then include your classes and who your
teachers were. It is quite possible, if your teacher has professional theatre experience, that their name will be known by
some directors. The theatre world is very small.

A casting director or producer is going to look at your résumé,
and I can tell you that at least in the case of the casting director
if there is *any* reason at all not to look at a résumé – because it
is hard to decipher owing either to poor font choice or to too
much crammed onto the page – they are going to throw it into
the trash. This is also true of auditors who may have an interest
in you because they have seen you do a promising audition, but
are then faced with a piece of paper listing what you have done
in such haphazard, overdone haste (which reads as desperate)
that they are forced to shake their head. You don't' want them
to shake their head, unless it is because you are so darn good
on that stage.

The point is to proudly and cleanly list what you have done,
no matter how much of a beginner you may be or how unim-
pressive you think your fledgling credits may be. Everybody has
to start somewhere. In any event it will not be necessary to list
all of your acting jobs. That can look desperate as well. As your
career gets started you will add more and it will go through
many changes, as mine has. You will also want to look at it again
from time to time to make sure you are still showing them what
you want to show them. Good credits can be listed so poorly
that they look like bad credits, and meager credits skillfully presented can look like great credits. So be ever vigilant about this
piece of paper meant to represent you in your absence. And
one more thing: never *ever* lie on a résumé!

YOUR NAME

Union Affiliation if Any
Home Phone #   Height
Cell Phone #   Eye Color
Email Address   Hair Color

THEATRE ROLES YOU HAVE PLAYED

PLAY   Character   Theatre Company

PLAY	Character	Theatre Company
PLAY	Character	Theatre Company
PLAY	Character	Theatre Company
PLAY	Character	Theatre Company
PLAY	Character	Theatre Company
PLAY	Character	Theatre Company
PLAY	Character	Theatre Company
PLAY	Character	Theatre Company

FILM/TV ROLES YOU HAVE PLAYED

FILM	Character	Film/TV Company
FILM	Character	Film/TV Company
FILM	Character	Film/TV Company
FILM	Character	Film/TV Company

TRAINING YOU HAVE HAD

SCHOOLS/ STUDIOS	Major/Degree	Years Attended

ACTING TEACHER(S)
VOICE TEACHER(S)
MOVEMENT TEACHER(S)
SPECIAL SKILLS – e.g. Juggling, Stage
Combat, Musical Instrument(s), etc.

INDEX

actual cue in a scene 154–5;
see also performance notes;
performance tips; rehearsal
notes
Dirt Cheap Headshots 189
dirty-word monologues 33
discoveries: "every line is a new
discovery" exercise 76–7;
during monologues 3, 67–8
'doing too much' 134, 163; *see
also* "less is more" note
downstage 62–3, 173; *see also*
below
drama: actions for 74–5; crying
and yelling 105–6; dramatic
dialogues 24–5; "play a
comedy like a tragedy and a
tragedy like a comedy" 104,
148, 152
The Drama Book Shop 182
Dramatic Publishing 182
Dramatist's Play Service 182
dress and hygiene (at auditions)
112–13; for men 111; for
women 112; *see also* clothing
dress rehearsals 140
Durang, Christopher: *Dentity
Crisis* 23; *Laughing Wild* 23

Elice, Rick, *Peter and the
Starcatcher* (scene 7) 92–3
ellipsis/dash 146–7
ELT (Equity Library Theatre) 71
emotion: how to play it 135; let
the audience do the feeling 146
Emotional Groupings 61
end (of monologue
presentation) 68–9; *see also*
exit (from audition room)

ends of words and consonants
159
entrance (at auditions) 115
Equity Library Theatre (ELT) 71
Equity Principal Auditions 2
"every line is a new discovery"
exercise 76–7
exercises 73–4, 76; "become
the monologue" 82–3;
"beginning, middle, end"
83–5; "every line is a new
discovery" 76–7; "hit the
deck" 64, 80–1; "make them
believe you" 77–8; "one-word
beat change" 81–2; "rooting
for gold" 77; "shout, then
whisper" 79; "sing, then Ha!"
79–80; "vowel thru" 78–9; *see
also* actions
exit (from audition room) 68–9,
100, 122
exit lines 147
explosions (blow-ups) 135–6
exposition 46, 173

fear of "I don't know!" 133–4
'feel sorry for yourself'
monologues 30–1
"female ingénue" roles 113
Field, Sally 5
fighting for something: and
cutting monologues 53;
and focus points 117; and
monologue definition 3;
and Neil Simon's characters
23; and 'one-person-show'
monologues 36; and
outrageous situations 11;
and 'remembering the

"leading lady/man" roles 113
"less is more" note 157–8; *see also* 'doing too much'
lights, at auditions 115–16
"like" filler word 131, 132
Lindsay-Abaire, *Rabbit Hole* 23
listening 155–6
Little Shop of Horrors (musical film) 128
Lloyd-Williams, *Actions: The Actor's Thesaurus* (Calderone and Lloyd-Williams) 61
Logan, John, *Red* (scene 4) 88–9
looking down: don't look down for too long 145–6; *see also* 'cheating up'; "Up Good, Down Bad"
"Looking Good" (George Wojtasik), and showcase productions 71
looks: and types of roles 18–19; *see also* clothing; tattoos
'losing it' 135–6
"louder, faster, funnier" note 164–5
love: and anger 24, 72, 88; and bombast 93; and cutting monologues 53–4, 56; and imagination 10; look for expression of 107; in love with being in love 91; and "objective is not big enough" pitfall 89; and outrageous situations 7, 8–11; self-love 72, 166; and thoughtfulness 90–1
"Lucy's Famous Chocolate Scene" 104–5
Ludwig, Ken 23

McNally, Terrence 23
"make them believe you" exercise 77–8
"male ingénu" roles 113
Mamet, David 25; *American Buffalo* 33
Man of La Mancha (musical) 33
Marceau, Marcel 66
'meeting the play on its terms' 139–40
memorization 51–2
men: men's clothing for auditions 111; monologue suggestions for 178–9; monologue suggestions for African-Americans 180
metaphors: journey metaphor 106–7; vs simile 132
The Method 174
middle (of monologue presentation) 67–8
MidWest Theatre Auditions 186
Miller, Arthur 24; *The Crucible* 153; *Death of a Salesman* 10, 29, 80, 82–3, 145, 148
miming: don't mime 66; and phone-call monologues 30
Modernage 188–9
Molière, *The Miser* 10
moment-to-moment playing 144
monologues: definition 3–4; monologue progression 53, *54*, 56, 59–60, 61; as outrageous situations 4, 7–12, 171; sixty-second monologues 1–2, 110–11; soliloquies 3, 4, 11, 100–1, 117; suggestion lists 177–80; *see also* choosing

screenplay monologues 35–6, 100

Seesaw (musical) 32

self-love 72, 166

self-pity, and 'feel sorry for yourself' monologues 30–1

servant roles 144

SETC (Southeastern Theatre Conference) 14, 109, 185–6

sex appeal, and Type 113

sexuality, and Type 113

sexually explicit language 33

Shakespeare, William: and antithesis 69–70, 71; to avoid for auditions 37–8; and "become the monologue" exercise 82; and crowd noise 144–5; and "just say it" 158; and new/nonsense words 159–60; servant roles 144; and sounding realistic 138; and speaking to the audience 3

Shakespeare plays: *Antony and Cleopatra* 43; *As You Like It* 112, 149; *The Comedy of Errors* 144, 156; *Hamlet* 12, 71, 147, 166; *Henry V* 117, 152; *King Lear* 148; *Macbeth* 26, 137, 144; *The Merry Wives of Windsor* 97; *A Midsummer Night's Dream* vi; *Much Ado about Nothing* 64; *Othello* 139, 156; *Romeo and Juliet* 9–10, 90–1, 125, 171; *The Taming of the Shrew* 139; *The Tempest* 170; *Timon of Athens* 72; *Titus Andronicus* 128; *The Two Gentlemen of Verona* 32

Shanley, John Patrick 25, 28

Shaw, George Bernard 38; *Mrs. Warren's Profession* 139

Shonge, Ntozage, *for colored girls* 24

"shout, then whisper" exercise 79

showcase productions, "Looking Good" at 71

"side kick" roles 113

simile, vs metaphor 132

Simon, Neil: *Barefoot in the Park* 23, 103; *Biloxi Blues* 23; *Brighton Beach Memoirs* 23, 103–4; *Broadway Bound* 23; *Chapter Two* 23, 32; *The Last of the Red Hot Lovers* 23; *The Odd Couple* 23, 30; *The Prisoner of Second Avenue* 23; *Star-Spangled Girl* 23

"sing, then Ha!" exercise 79–80

sixty-second auditions 1–2, 13–16, 103, 110–11, 171; *see also* auditions; audition step by step

Skinner, Edith 150, 173

slating (film acting) 117

Smith and Kraus Monologues 182, 183

soliloquies 3, 4, 11, 100–1, 117

songs: auditioning for 14; as monologues 11, 12; 'too much out of context' songs 34; 'what a screw-up I am' songs 32–3; *see also* musicals

Sophocles, *Oedipus the King* 10, 106, 128

The Sound of Music (musical) 12

Southeastern Theatre Conference (SETC) 14, 109, 185–6

Printed in the USA
CPSIA information can be obtained
at www.ICGtesting.com
LVHW011605231023
761906LV00009B/276